Dear God,
I feel like
a whale!

Knowing
God's touch
throughout
your pregnancy
– and beyond

Jane Bullivant

MONARCH
BOOKS

Oxford, UK, and Grand Rapids, Michigan

First published in the UK by Monarch Books
(a publishing imprint of Lion Hudson plc),
Mayfield House, 256 Banbury Road, Oxford OX2 7DH
Tel: +44 (0) 1865 302750 Fax: +44 (0) 1865 302757
Email: monarch@lionhudson.com
www.lionhudson.com

UK ISBN 1 85424 661 5
US ISBN 0 8254 6066 2

Distributed by:
UK: Marston Book Services Ltd, PO Box 269,
Abingdon, Oxon OX14 4YN;
USA: Kregel Publications, PO Box 2607,
Grand Rapids, Michigan 49501.

British Library Cataloguing Data
A catalogue record for this book is available
from the British Library.

Printed and bound in Great Britain by
Bookmarque Ltd, Croydon, Surrey

Contents

Acknowledgements

Yippee! I hollered as the 50,000th word landed on my laptop and this book was finally finished. It was such a momentous moment that I paused, almost expecting the world to stop spinning just for a moment...

"MUM, MY BIKE'S STUCK IN THE THORNS!"

Dreams of authorship forgotten, I dashed outside to see Joseph and Samuel valiantly disentangling a bike from the world's thorniest raspberry bush. At that same moment Miranda (baby number three) began to wail for a feed and the freezer door burst open, spilling frozen peas everywhere. Welcome to my world. Not one of an "author" but of a young mum who has lots of fun, makes lots of mistakes and spends her days chasing after three turbo-charged kids and stuffing more in a freezer than is humanly possible.

First, I must thank my kind-hearted and mischievous husband without whom this book would not have been written, because I am the most computer illiterate person ever to write a book. I only worked out how to transfer a file last week, and don't even ask me what a D drive is. Thank you to my three wonderful kids, Joseph, Samuel and Miranda. May this book always remind you that you are treasured beyond measure, and to chase with all your hearts after what is good and true.

Before I was a Bullivant I was a Cartwright – so I'd like to thank my mum for showing me what unconditional love is all about. Dad, your hunger for knowing God in day-to-day life is so contagious. Thanks to my sister Andrea – your stunning beauty of heart has inspired so much hope in this book. My brother Stephen, you are a God-chaser and your Elijah heart has shaped the writing of this book too. Heather and Ryder, you have run the race and inspired us all to dig deep and run for God, whether or not the crowds cheer.

I'd like to thank Tristan and Alison Harris for your support during our early years of parenthood which enabled me to receive God's healing. Your compassion had a huge impact on my mothering. A big thank you to all the precious mums who shared their stories for the final chapter. Special thanks to Martine Woodbridge, Danielle Vaughan and Gemma Brown. You are sunbeams from heaven!

Thank you to my editors Tony Collins and Eleanor Trotter and the fantastic team at Monarch.

Finally, this book is dedicated to the memory of my cousin Rachel, a young mum who knew what it was to lift up her head and trust the living God: "Don't just exist. LIVE!" (Rachel Covington)

Jane Bullivant
May 2004

Foreword

I well remember the joy and fear, the excitement and dis-
comfort of my first pregnancy. Thirty years ago, there were
few books about what was going on inside a mother's body,
and even fewer about what was happening in her mind and
emotions. I clung to a tiny booklet lent to me by a friend, a
very limited source of medical information, but all I had. I
especially needed something written from a Christian view-
point which could help me to pray, and to evaluate my coming role of motherhood from God's perspective, but I looked
in vain for some help on the shelves of a Christian bookshop
for any kind of spiritual advice.

Pregnancy was new territory. Everything was strange:
one's body gained alarming new contours, emotions swung
from elation to despair, and suddenly coffee and the smell of
frying bacon produced unbearable nausea. In fact just walking into Sainsbury's and seeing and smelling the raw meat
was an ordeal!

There were days when I was excited, full of joyful anticipation, but also many when I was unsure and afraid. As my
girth expanded, I lived in one secondhand maternity dress
and an adapted garment that had belonged to my husband's
overweight aunt! One day, trying to get ready for a wedding,
I caught sight of my swollen body in the mirror, and, transfixed with horrified fascination, I burst into tears. I felt

ungainly, clumsy and uncomfortable... How young mums need encouragement and affirmation!

Each pregnancy is a new miracle, and should hold wonder and an extraordinary sense of privilege that a new human being is being formed in one's body. If you are a Christian, there is a new awareness of the power and tenderness of our Creator as he knits this new life together, and a kind of amazement that we are cooperating with him as he does so. How extremely sad then that there are many young women with little support during such a crucial time, and increasingly many who are unwilling participators in this great process.

My fifth and last pregnancy was unplanned, and therefore a shock. It enabled me to identify somewhat with those for whom pregnancy is a seeming disaster. However, when my doctor mentioned that I might have grounds for a termination, my reaction was one of total revulsion. I was surprised at how violent my feelings were. I realised how desperate a woman must be to go through with such a thing, as it violates something deeply imbedded in the depths of her being. My instinct to cling on to the embryonic life was far stronger than my reluctance to carry it.

How fortunate I was to be married to a man committed to me and committed to God. Together we prayed and trusted God for the strength and resources to bring this child to birth and raise him. Today he is 22 years old and a trainee teacher, and life would be unthinkable without him!

Having experienced pregnancy, and given birth five times, I am well aware of the tensions, anxieties, fear and joy that are generated by these unique yet common events. A book from someone who has been there and walked through it several times, upheld by the strength and love of God, is long overdue. Jane empathises, with humour, common sense and practical wisdom, but also from a spiritual perspective. I welcome this book and I know it will be grabbed eagerly by many mothers-to-be. They will laugh and cry their way through it, and feel a reassuring arm around their shoulders. As Isaiah 40:11 puts it so eloquently, "He tends his flock like a shepherd, he gathers the lambs in his arms, and carries them close to his heart; he gently leads those that have young."

Wendy Virgo
May 2004

Chapter 1   "Oops, I Told the Doughtnut-seller"

If your childhood memories are like watching a rerun of *The Simpsons*, then at least you'll know how you DON'T want to do parenthood. If your memories, like mine, are more reminiscent of the family in *The Waltons*, then you might have an idea of exactly how you DO want to do parenthood. However, making the jump from being a fiery, life-loving vixen with a partiality to microwave meals to the apple-pie-baking perfection of my mother still has me flummoxed. Even when I gleefully let it slip to the doughnut-seller that I was, in fact, pregnant, I still couldn't shake off those lingering questions that had hung around ever since we decided to have a baby. "Have we made the right decision?" "What about the pain?" "What if I'm not ready to be a mum?" This sort of life-changing decision is never easy; I find it tricky enough deciding between chow mein and chop suey at Mr Wong's.

For many of us, any of the dilemmas that may surround the decision to start a family simply aren't in the picture. Pregnancy tends to happen just when you are in the middle of rebuilding the kitchen, starting the job of your dreams, or looking forward to being your sister's bridesmaid. Planned or not, when the impossible happens, the thought of taking a peep into your baby's secret world suddenly becomes madly intriguing. Becoming a mum brings with it a sort of thrill/ panic combination that reminds me of the exhilarating yet scary rush of childhood adventures. Having a baby has got to be the ultimate roller coaster of excitement, fears and dreams.

Confessions of a duvet-hogger

Being hijacked by your rampant hormones and finding yourself weepy or hungry most of the time is quite a wake-up call even for the most maternal of us. There's a constant feeling that life is never going to be quite the same again; that kooky combination of fear and spine-tingling anticipation. Most of us develop a whole new hobby: lying awake wondering, planning, and demanding the entire duvet. I also had quite an impressive repertoire of late-night ponderings. They included:

- Why did I break down in floods of tears when Captain Kirk died in *Star Trek*? I don't even like *Star Trek*.
- Why have I never realised before that curry with cottage cheese is so delicious?
- Why do my breasts now enter the room ten minutes before I do?

Occasionally, despite my hormone-hijacked state, I pondered more complex questions such as:

- How does my baby's heart start beating?
- How does each cell know what it is to become?
- When will my baby know my voice?

Finally, my burning questions were:

- WHY is there a new life?
- Could it really be true that my baby has a destiny?

- Could it be possible that God longs for this baby as much as I do?

Armed with such exciting thoughts, it can be tempting to imagine that your baby will be a serene little article who grows up to love church more than chocolate and wants to become the next Billy Graham or Mother Teresa. Indeed, you may be one of the lucky few. The rest of us find ourselves with a wriggling, sleep-defying individual who develops into an excitable, carpet-biting toddler who grows up wanting to be an astronaut. As I squeeze my huge pregnant bump in front of the laptop (baby number three on the way), it's rather mind-blowing even to think that the same hands that flung stars into space now tenderly shape my little one. Awesome.

Did you not pour me out like milk and curdle me like cheese, clothe me with skin and flesh and knit me together with bones and sinews? You gave me life... (Job 10:10–12).

That moment of truth

You'll never forget that moment when you found out that you were pregnant for the first time. I skulked off to the bathroom with the testing kit convinced it would be negative and I should have bought a lipstick instead. The magic blue line appeared on the test and before I knew it I was sobbing into the shag pile in amazement, delight and sheer panic. In the days that followed, my husband kept asking me if I felt nauseous. As I didn't feel sick, I started secretly congratulating myself that maybe this was nature's way of letting me know I would be a natural mother. I wasn't smug for long. One evening I opened a can of tuna and got a whiff of watery fish.

I then found myself making a dash for the back door making noises like a dog trying to get up a sharp piece of bone. That was pretty much the story for the next six weeks. Somewhat tricky to carry on as normal when you feel rough and you're bursting with the most earth-shattering secret that you're HAVING A BABY.

When you do find out that there's a baby on the way, you quickly realise that it has got to be one of the hardest secrets in the world to keep. When you're bursting with such news, it really is tempting to let it slip to the doughnut-seller. My plan to tell my husband involved writing "I'M PREGNANT!" in a cute card and burying it under the lakeside log where we had our wedding photos taken. Then I planned to set up some kind of treasure hunt for him to find it. I imagined that he would whoop with delight and whisk me off for a celebratory meal. What actually happened, aside from it pouring with rain, was that he rang up from work to ask if he'd had any phone calls, and I couldn't resist blurting it out

The biggest secret ever

I remember my early weeks of pregnancy as a frenzy of parsnip sandwiches, multiple bathroom trips and giddy visits to the baby goods shop. My whirlwind was perhaps only tempered by a new-found awe at my enlarging breasts. In the midst of all this activity, I stumbled on something that stopped me in my tracks. It all started when I was kept waiting in the doctor's surgery as I queued to register my pregnancy. I suddenly remembered that I would get asked the date of my last period. I guessed saying that it was the day I lost my keys wouldn't really do. Then, as I mentally tried to work out what that date must have been, when IT must have happened, and how long I'd actually been pregnant, I realised something rather earth-shattering. Until I did that pregnancy test, I had had no clue that I had a whole new life growing inside me. But God knew. This new life was his secret. His very real hand was on a very real me, tenderly shaping a new life, and I didn't even know it! How totally intimate. It really caught my breath then, as it still does even now:

> My frame was not hidden from you when I was made in the secret place...your eyes saw my unformed body (Psalm 139:15,16).

A chink of heaven

There's something very special about being pregnant that is so much more than just having a baby. It's like taking a peek into eternity and seeing a chink of heaven. God the creator, right here and now. It's a window of opportunity to meet God in a whole new way. Arriving home from the doctor's surgery that blustery afternoon, I made a decision. Tempting as it was to slob around in the evenings swigging neat antacid and reading baby magazines, I decided to spend some time seeking God during my pregnancy. That was six years and four pregnancies ago. I have grappled with the Bible and spent long nights feeding my babies and seeking God. I have seen his touch on my little ones. Knowing God's touch on your family is the trek of a lifetime into new territory, and I'm still only just getting my boots on.

Does my bum look big in this?

I confess that during the following long haul of the first trimester, I changed from a lively, friendly sort of girl to more of a grumpy madam with a freaky cleanliness habit. My friends found my grumpiness quite amusing. In fact, I felt like a moody teenager all over again. Only this time I wasn't just looking in the mirror wondering if my bum was getting bigger – it was growing before my very eyes.

During my teenage years I think I spent half of my time looking in the mirror and the other half on my brother's Game Boy® playing Tetris. Sad, but true. I even took the Game Boy® to church with me. I remember one half-empty church service when I was in the back row as usual, Game Boy® in hand, watching the clock. After the final rousing hymn there was a short time of prayer. My dad got up and mumbled a few words of thanks, then prayed for healing for a long-standing member of the church who had been paralysed for years. I was so embarrassed. Never had "prayer for the sick" happened in our sleepy church before, and my dad had only been a Christian for three months. I was mortified, and carried on playing on the Game Boy®. Well, gingerly the paralysed lady actually rose to her feet and walked. There wasn't a TV evangelist in sight! Everyone in the church, and later the entire town, was open-mouthed. The doctors later confirmed by scan that new nerves had grown. It was obvious to even us cynical teenagers in the back row that here was a very real God, with very real involvement in normal people's lives. God just reached down and restored without razzle-dazzle or fanfare. In that moment of renewal I saw for real the raw beauty of God the restorer, deliverer and creator.

During pregnancy we have two options when it comes to our walk with God:

1. We could just try and get through pregnancy, and put our Christian life on the back burner.

OR we can

2.   Put down our Game Boy® consoles and watch the miracle happening right in front of our eyes.

Do you catch my drift?

Let's drag our attention away from all the stuff that fills our lives and give 100% of our attention to the miracle-maker with his hand on our tummies. Knowing God's touch when you have a baby is not some feel-good woolly talk. It is as real as the baby you love.

Nailing the fear gremlins

Perhaps one of the biggest obstacles to be overcome when it comes to enjoying your miracle is the fear of what could happen. Some of us have had previous experience of difficult pregnancies, difficult births, or even lost babies. There is a rut of fear that can seem impossible to contemplate getting out of and, before we know it, we've been robbed of a peaceful entry into motherhood. I know this one well, having had a miscarriage, fulminating pre-eclampsia, an emergency Caesarean, a baby in the neonatal unit with breathing problems, and heart problems myself. I guess that if I learned anything through it all, it is this: I want to put my unborn baby's life in God's hands and trust him for whatever hurdles we may face. I think the best love we can give our babies is not one that suffocates or is tinged with fear. The best love we can give is one that is confident that God is faithful. Then we can love freely, because the reality is that God loves them even more than we do.

No guts, no glory

I know of a young mother who, when it came to the crunch, was confident in God's faithfulness to her little one. She wrapped her three-month-old baby up in his favourite blanket, with his arm out of the sheet so that he could reach his thumb. Kissing him tenderly on his dark, fuzzy head, she laid him in his basket. As he flashed a gurgling smile at her she trusted God for his life. Her story is one of the most amazing I have ever read...

(Don't skip this bit!)

...Pharaoh gave this order to all his people: "Every boy that is born you must throw into the Nile, but let every girl live."

Now a man of the house of Levi married a Levite woman, and she became pregnant and gave birth to a son. When she saw that he was a fine child, she hid him for three months. But when she could hide him no longer, she got a papyrus basket for him and coated it with tar and pitch. Then she placed the child in it and put it among the reeds along the banks of the Nile. His sister stood at a distance to see what would happen to him. Then Pharaoh's daughter went down to the Nile to bathe, and her attendants were walking along the river bank. She saw the basket among the reeds and sent her slave girl to get it. She opened it and saw the baby. He was crying, and she felt sorry for him. "This is one of the Hebrew babies," she said.

Then his sister asked Pharaoh's daughter, "Shall I go and get one of the Hebrew women to nurse the baby for you?"

"Yes, go," she answered. And the girl went and got the

baby's mother. Pharaoh's daughter said to her, "Take this baby and nurse him for me, and I will pay you." So the woman took the baby and nursed him. When the child grew older, she took him to Pharaoh's daughter and he became her son. She named him Moses... (Exodus 1:22 – 2:10).

How did this young mother have the guts to really let her baby go and trust God? I suspect it is because she knew that God stays faithful even when circumstances seem to fall apart. She trusted her Father God, no questions asked. So, what became of baby Moses? He became the leader of Israel, a man who met face to face with God on the top of a mountain, a hero who negotiated the release of millions of slaves. The nuts and bolts of it all is that if you too become a mum who trusts in your God, and you have the guts to walk with him every day, Jesus himself will come and be with your family. As a Garfield cartoon once said, "No guts, no glory".

True to character

My brother has a friend who is renowned for his practical jokes. So impressive is his reputation, that, when he announced his intention to marry, he and his fiancé were quite apprehensive as to what his smug friends might plan for the wedding day. Surprisingly, the wedding passed without a hitch, and the relieved newlyweds assumed that their friends hadn't got around to hatching any plots. During the evening wedding party, the thought crossed the groom's mind that his friends would never miss an opportunity like this to play a joke. He knew them too well. Yet nothing happened. Eventually the evening drew to a close and the newlyweds retired to the hotel's honeymoon suite for their wedding night. The next morning, they phoned room service and asked for two continental breakfasts. As they did so, a voice from nowhere added, "Make that three!" Lo and behold, the groom's best friend had actually spent the night under their bed!

The groom knew all too well what his friends were really like. Despite the circumstances appearing to suggest that they hadn't played a joke, they had indeed stayed true to their characters. All the time we confidently rely on people's characters, and we base a lot of decisions on what we believe about people we hardly know. Yet God is a thousand times more reliable. His character is unswervingly faithful. We can rely on it and know that he will not act out of character. He never does. If you cry out to him for your new family, he will always hear your every word.

Treacle pudding and Marmite

It has been said that for sperm to reach the egg, they have to face the equivalent of paddling through an ocean of treacle. But what a jackpot for the winner! Then the miracle explosion begins as the cells divide and grow like lightning. Potential with a capital "P". We have also been given a new season, a fresh start. It's not too late to start talking to God more; it's not too late to be all that God intended you to be.

Every baby book that you lay your hands on will enthuse about the importance of eating a well-balanced diet with plenty of fresh fruit and vegetables. However, the simple truth is that it is almost impossible to eat the right amounts, of the right foods, all of the time. When you wake in the middle of the night fantasising about treacle pudding smeared with Marmite, all the rules go out of the window. Even so, it can be very tempting, when you are pregnant, to jump on the bandwagon and put loads of effort into staying physically healthy while leaving your walk with God (spiritual health) on the shelf. It's easy to miss your chance for a fresh start, to put your godly potential on the back burner.

Well, if you're just setting off on the jungle track of pregnancy, or if you're further on up its adventurous trail, there are four golden nuggets that might make your journey easier and safer. Think of them as four chocolate bars for your backpack.

1. Eat well!
A varied diet is best. This includes a balance of fresh fruit and vegetables, carbohydrates and proteins. That's what the books tell you. Me? Well, as a connoisseur of parsnip sandwiches and mushroom korma with cheese when pregnant, I don't know whether I'm qualified to comment. I'd be the last to deny you your latest fondant delicacy; I suppose variety is the key.

2. Drink lots of water!
Drinking plenty of fluids each day will cleanse your body and provide the extra needed for the baby. In my pre-pregnancy days I was an avid tea drinker, yet for some reason tea tasted like old cheese when I was pregnant. Fortunately, I discovered the delights of pure-fruit smoothies. Almost as good as sex.

3. Try to get some rest during the day!
If you have another child, getting rest during the day is likely to be snatching ten minutes' sit-down while *Winnie the Pooh* is on TV, or pretending to play sleeping lions just so you can lie down uninterrupted for a few moments. If you're at work, let delegation become your new best friend.

4. Don't miss the boat!

> Jesus answered, "Everyone who drinks this water will be thirsty again, but whoever drinks the water I give him will never thirst. Indeed, the water I give him will become in him a spring of water welling up into eternal life" (John 4:13–14).

Drink deep while you can. Now is your season to reach your potential in God. As the bumper sticker says, "Eternal life isn't pie in the sky when you die. It's steak on the plate while you wait!"

Time out with your Father God

> For you created my inmost being; you knit me together in my mother's womb. I praise you because I am fearfully and wonderfully made; your works are wonderful, I know that full well. My frame was not hidden from you when I was made in the secret place. When I was woven together in the depths of the earth, your eyes saw my unformed body. All the days ordained for me were written in your book before one of them came to be (Psalm 139:13–16).

Below are some thoughts I had when I found out that I was pregnant with my first baby, Joseph. Why not use the space underneath to write a letter or poem to God of your own that expresses where you're at right now.

New creation

Nestled in the palm of the living God is my precious secret.
Tenderly, God designs, shapes and invigorates,
He is preparing a destiny of life and discovery.
Holding the hand of the living God...
What a privilege I carry!
I soar on wings like eagles.
Precious Holy Spirit, hold me, refresh me,
Shape my heart also, make it yours.
Tenderly, I carry this child,
The Father's desired inheritance.
O little one, so fragile,
Your Creator is so faithful.
He is your sustainer, your provider,
Your tiny hand in his.

(Jane, five weeks pregnant)

Chapter 2   # Stockpiling Mum-wisdom

Mention the words "water birth" to my friend and she glazes over like a teenager in a bus queue. In her opinion, a "surrender-to-it" natural birth is just too organic and chancy. I'm sure she's convinced that it would involve her obstetrician wearing cute little Armani trunks, and her husband watching and cheering like he did when he saw the whales at Sea World. Ask my friend Ruth, however, who gave birth to Alex in a birth pool at home last week, and the picture is very different. Her birth was relaxed and cosy and over in less than three hours. She said that the warmth of the water was so soothing that she nodded off between contractions. The atmosphere was very friendly; even the midwives were nibbling on doughnuts.

Decisions, decisions

We all have such different thoughts on what an "ideal birth" is, and it's easy to catch yourself thinking about IT quite often. The first step is choosing where to have your baby. "Choice" is the buzzword in maternity care these days, and there is certainly plenty of it. You'll also be asked whether you want antenatal screening or not, and whom you want as birth companions, and that's just for starters. Then, of course, there are choices to be made about what type of cot and car seat you buy – not forgetting decisions about work and finances. With so many choices to consider, it's no wonder that even the most maternal of us find ourselves diving for the remote control for some quiz-show therapy. In this unending, yet strangely exciting, whirlwind of decisions, it can be such a huge relief if you can get some honest advice from someone who really understands your situation.

Nuggets of wisdom

Your midwife and obstetrician are certainly top-notch resources for all kinds of advice. They are especially good for those burning questions that you lie awake thinking about, convincing yourself they are far too silly to mention. Friends who have had children have a fantastic stockpile of pregnancy wisdom, although the "warts and all" honesty can be quite a wake-up call when you've been hijacked by your hormones. Your own mum, or older women you know, might also offer a wide selection of nuggets of wisdom, some of which will be real lifesavers. If you can pinpoint a few of these people that you really trust, then you'll definitely feel as if you can surf the choppy waves of decision-making and actually come out the other end home and dry.

Stockpiling wisdom from health professionals

Your midwife or obstetrician will be a key player in the coming months, and your first port of call. On the offchance, however, that you realise that you can't stand the one assigned to you (or she's your neighbour or something), you can see if you can trade her in for another one. Most health professionals rate highly in the information- and advice-giving stakes; they will be in their element if you ask them for a run-down of what services are available in your area.

Parentcraft classes

The very name of these classes conjures up visions of bootee-knitting lessons and embarrassing role-playing exercises. When my friend's husband realised that you were expected to take a pillow, he was convinced it would be some kind of touchy-feely lovefest, and she had to bribe him with a new DVD to get him to come. I can see where he's coming from: it certainly looks as if there's an all-night party going on as twelve couples shuffle down the hospital corridor with pillows tucked under their arms. Being faced with the option of clutching your forget-me-not pillow, or carrying your handbag so that you can carry your pillow, is enough to send most men hot-footing it back to the car. If you do make it down the corridor, these classes can be really worth going to and a great chance to meet people going through similar experiences to you.

Walking, nay, skipping out of my first prenatal appointment, I was so excited about getting home to read all the pregnancy literature stuffed in my bag. My bubble of anticipation burst as I started leafing through the limp pamphlets. I'm sure that I'm not the first woman to have a problem with the standard-issue pregnancy leaflets and books. Phrases like "morning nausea" were way off the mark in describing the heaving sensation I felt at the sight of a tin of tuna. "Appetite may increase slightly" was nothing like the words I'd use to describe my thoughts when we drove past an Indian takeaway one night. (I had jumped out of the car at the traffic lights because I ABSOLUTELY HAD TO HAVE a mushroom korma.) To real women going through it, even the tiniest pregnancy symptoms are a big deal. This is only really understood by women who've been through it too, women like your friends.

Stockpiling pregnancy wisdom from friends

Your friends will give you the real story, haemorrhoids and all (prepare yourself). They will have no problem in telling you that having huge boobs does not make you look like Lara Croft, and that half your pregnancy wardrobe makes you look fat rather than pregnant. Try not to pick a friend who is known for embellishing stories, or you might find yourself dashing out of the coffee shop to your obstetrician's office and begging for a Caesarean (as if THAT'S the easy option!). Being pregnant is like joining a street gang. You're one of "them" now. Even strangers in the park will assume that you'll want to hear every grisly detail of their birth, their neighbour's horror story, and about a friend who buried her placenta under her rockery. There will be nuggets of wisdom hidden somewhere amongst the flurry of opinions offered by friends. Here's a recent example... I read the other day in a pregnancy book that rucksacks, worn loosely, are a sensible way of carrying things about when you're pregnant. Something to do with the weight being equally balanced between both shoulders. Seemed to make sense to me. Just as I had picked out a trendy suede rucksack, my wise friend casually commented that a rogue rucksack strap would probably end up lassoing one of my enormous breasts. Good point.

Your own usually reliable gut instinct can sometimes go a bit haywire when you're pregnant. My friend Ruth from Denver, USA was convinced that there were lots of bacteria on her light switches. Positive that she could simply not be pregnant in a home with such filth, she set to work on the light switches with bleach and a toothbrush. I laugh at this, but I do confess that when I'm pregnant I find myself holding my breath when I empty the bin or bleach the drain. I remember my friend Pam balanced precariously on the kitchen table, nine months pregnant, ferociously stencilling apples round the kitchen wall as though her life depended on it. This nesting instinct on turbo boost is up there with crazy food fads, birth stories, hospital stories, and insomnia tales as the top five stories your friends will happily share with you.

Stockpiling wisdom from experienced mums

The experiences of your mother, or of other older women in your church are not to be politely ignored. True, they may think that epidural is some kind of motor oil and meconium is a new brand of instant coffee. They may not have heard of the NCT, Leboyer, La Leche League or any other popular birthing trend. However, older women will usually be keen to hear all about your pregnancy symptoms and baby plans, which is always nice. Let's face it: a captive audience for your incessant pregnancy chatter may well be in short supply by now – time to widen the net. A definite bonus when you're flagging is that they might just take you under their wing for some home-made carrot cake. Nice. If you are already inclined to be sentimental in your progesterone-overloaded state, a chat with one of these women after church may almost make you consider inviting her to the birth out of thankfulness (I said *almost*).

The nuts and bolts of motherhood

The Bible talks about older women teaching younger women the nuts and bolts of motherhood. We're not talking how to knit a matinée jacket (please, no!) or even how to get a baby to sleep. I mean learning how to have a Christian foundation to your home, and how to raise a child in peace when the world around is in chaos.

When I was 15 and my sister was 18, we decided that our mum was her own worst enemy. She was always running around after our dad, us children and the housework, and she hardly had any time for herself. Even then she did cross-stitch pictures for other people! My sister and I decided that you couldn't sur-vive as a woman like that these days; you'd end up getting taken for granted.

Now here I am a few years later, about to get married, and I am so, so grateful for the example my mum set of investing herself in our family. The foundation of unconditional love that she laid gave us self-worth, security and confidence. The prior-ity she put on loving my dad before herself has shown me what marriage is all about.

(Andrea, 27)

Andrea's mum is precious. Unfortunately our generation doesn't seem to be following many positive choices made by the generation before us. If our generation had a motto, I reckon it would be "every woman for herself". More often than not, motherhood is at the bottom of the pile. Individualism is the name of the game. I think we should invest in a bit of wisdom from past generations and remem-ber that motherhood is one of the highest callings there is.

She is their earth... she is their food and their bed and the extra blanket when it grows cold in the night; she is their warmth and their health and their shelter.

(Katherine Butler Hathaway)

Gut-instinct wisdom

You are your baby's universe. It is impossible to grasp your value to him from the first moment he peers at you in the delivery room. Right from that moment, your own maternal instinct becomes a crucial part of the picture.

The first thing I noticed about my screaming bundle of life was the length of his fingers. I found myself thinking "Oh, he'll probably be good at the guitar one day" as if I was thinking about someone I knew really well. It was something I just can't explain, like falling in love across a crowded room, and wanting never to shut my eyes in case the magic disappeared. He knew it was me. Even light, clothing and noise seemed an intrusion. Oh yes, his smell, his smell. He clung to me like he felt safe. After the rocky journey of carrying him, I really felt like we'd reached the top of a mountain. We'd made it.

These were my thoughts after giving birth to our second baby, Samuel Alexander, which I scribbled down on the back of a hospital menu card.

Knowing what your baby wants

At first, knowing what your baby wants when he or she cries is really tricky. That's the point at which breastfeeding can come into its own as an instant comforter, regardless of when the last "feed" was – and you barely have to wake up! As the days go by, all mums gradually get attuned to their baby's needs and become quite an expert on their own little one. Women's instincts are different, and so are the babies we care for.

When our baby was born it felt totally right to tuck our new baby in bed with us at night. It was real bonding time and had the added bonus that I didn't even have to get out of my bed to feed him. Unfortunately, I made the mistake of telling people, and everyone told me that I was making a rod for my own back;

he would never sleep through the night. Suddenly, I lost all my
confidence, assuming that everyone else knew better than me.
So we moved him to his cot. The well-meaning advice was prob-
ably partly right; we probably did have more broken nights
than other people when we moved him to his cot. Even so, I still
don't regret going with my instinct and I wish we'd stuck to our
guns more.

(Anonymous, happy mum of three)

The reality is that what works for one family may not be ideal
for the next family. (A point to note here is that an adult who
has been drinking or has taken medication should never
share a bed with a baby or child.) The crucial thing is making
an informed choice and then doing what you feel is right,
with confidence. It takes courage to be a parent; trust your
instinct, make use of some stockpiled wisdom, and then go
for it.

Stockpiling wisdom from heaven itself

Well, we've looked at stockpiling wisdom from health professionals, your friends, your mum and your own gut instinct.
So what's the deal with godly wisdom and life in the 21st cen-
tury – can they work together? Getting to grips with the topic
of godly wisdom can sound like a really heavyweight task,
best left to keen Bible-college students – certainly not to a
pregnant woman on her third sardine smoothie. Well, bear
with me; are you ready for a surprise?

Origami and loo-roll tubes

The other day, I came across some wisdom from *Dennis the
Menace*. In this cartoon episode, Dennis and his friend were
walking out of a neighbour's house clutching some snacks

that she had given them. They wondered what they had done to deserve the treats. Dennis concluded that they didn't get the snacks because they deserved them; it was simply because their neighbour was a kind lady. God doesn't dish out wisdom just to 10/10 Christians. He's our Father; he just loves to pour out wisdom to bless us because he loves us. Simple as that. Real wisdom comes from God, we can't "get wise" without him.

A wise mother is not so much one who can do origami with loo-roll tubes, or toilet-train a toddler, but one who can restore her household to peace when there is chaos. A wise mother has a real understanding of what life is about; no one pulls the wool over her eyes. When her children are teenagers, she knows when to let them learn consequences to their actions, and when to stop them before they get involved in the wrong thing. She covers her family in prayer, and through her example her family become Christians. Feeling daunted yet? Don't, because it's you I'm describing! If you turn your face to God and ask him to fill your heart with the things that move *his* heart, you will find yourself overflowing with his love, power and – you guessed it – wisdom!

> ...if my people, who are called by my name, will humble themselves and pray and seek my face...I...will heal their land (2 Chronicles 7:14).

Time to wise up

When you lay your heart in the fingertips of Almighty God and commit yourself to be the woman he created you to be, his glory will fall on your whole family. We all know it's not always easy; the key is to keep in step with God by reading the Bible – even if that does mean reading it in the bath because that's the only time you get to yourself. During the times when it feels like things are "not happening" with God, it's easy to wonder if he's even there. After all, the rest of the world seems to manage without him. The reality is that the rest of the world is not managing. Families are falling apart all over the place; children are growing up in a world full of insecurity and conflicting messages. Your family needs you. If you invest yourself in your family, learning your role under God, you are very likely to turn around your whole family's destiny.

Living life to the max

Saying the word "prayer" to many people is the quickest way to turn them off. Others can't help thinking of people in huddles in "the shampoo position", all trying not to fall asleep. In reality, this image is light years away from what prayer is all about. If you want to be a woman of God and grow in wisdom, simply walking and talking to God is the first place to start. If ever I begin to lose the plot about what prayer is really about, I stop and recall a boy I met a few years ago.

Ross was a fourteen-year-old boy in a youth group that I ran. He seemed to live for his electric guitar and CD collection. One youth group we had a discussion on prayer, and I asked the group to write on a piece of paper the word that they most connected with prayer. The answers predictably ranged from "God" to "communication". Ross wrote "*Pepsi Max*". When he showed me his answer I was puzzled, but before I had chance to ask him about it he had gone to catch his bus. Months later I happened to see the Pepsi advert – the image that was expressed was "*live life to the max*". Ross was really saying that prayer is awesome, and it enables us to live life to the max. Could he be right?

If you want wisdom, really want wisdom, taking time out with God is the thing to do. I've got a friend who listens to

God as he walks the dog every day. Having this routine has really helped him to keep listening to God every day. I have my "quiet time" in my noisy house as I wash up or do the ironing. Not as tranquil as a quiet garden bench (ours is currently in use as a toy-digger ramp), but then we've all got to start somewhere.

Hot tips for new mums

I'm just a wee young thing with loads to learn on the wise-mother front. However, I tracked down some experienced women of God for their best tips on godly wisdom for new mums...

Touch

This basic instinct, touch, is a really special channel of communication. Jesus even healed the sick by simply touching them.

> When the sun was setting, the people brought to Jesus all who had various kinds of sickness, and laying his hands on each one, he healed them (Luke 4:40).

Also, the woman with gynaecological problems...

> If I only touch his cloak, I will be healed (Matthew 9:21).

As soon as she touched the hem of Jesus' garment, the woman was cured.

Even without words, our touch can be a prayer of the heart, communicating God's love and power. Many of the women I spoke to said how precious it was for a mother to be open-hearted in a family and bless, comfort and reaffirm through touch. There is even scientific proof that premature babies put on weight faster, and fare better, if they have human touch. Here are some of the reasons why the wise mums I spoke to think it's a really good move to be open and demonstrative in your family:

- It demonstrates the unconditional acceptance and welcoming arms of Jesus
- It's warm, snuggly and fun
- It's a big world out there.

Little ones need reassuring that home is a safe and positive place to be. Let's make unconditional love the foundation of day-to-day life at home. I suspect it's one of the wisest moves we could ever make.

Companionship

One older mother told me that when she had her first baby she went to mother and baby groups and saw her neighbours and work colleagues, but inside she was desperately lonely. Having babies in common with other women wasn't enough to give real friendship. She said that if she had her time again she would make more of an effort to be a real and honest friend herself. There's nothing like a true friend when you've got a new baby. Real friendship is not meeting once a week, everyone saying that they're "fine", having a bit of a chat, then going home. Real friendship is about being honest, investing yourself in other people, crying with them, laughing with them and being real. Let's not settle for "friendship" that is anything less.

Expect the unexpected

Pregnancy can feel like such a roller-coaster ride, and it doesn't immediately stop when the baby is born, or even when she can talk. The wise mothers agreed unanimously that babies and children are not neat, predictable little packages. Somehow they've always got something up their sleeve that you weren't quite expecting. You just get the breastfeeding sorted out, and it's time to start weaning them onto food. You get that sorted, and then suddenly they're on the move. I think the moral of the story is to enjoy each stage, because it is over before you know it. It's really not worth getting stressed over each stage; just go with it. The wise women agreed that the future was a big unknown, and the thought of it was sometimes daunting. However, they unanimously concluded that they were actively equipping their children to make good choices and that they would always, always be there for them.

Time out with your Father God

Do you remember the film *Good Morning Vietnam!*? Robin Williams plays a radio DJ who starts his early morning show by yelling "GOOD MORNING, VIETNAM!" and waking the whole neighbourhood. Sometimes we too need a wake-up call, or life just passes us by. Why not try copying out the words below and sticking them on your fridge? Let it be your wake-up call. Root your heart in him. It's time to live!

> ...if my people, who are called by my name, will humble themselves and pray and seek my face and turn from their wicked ways, then will I hear from heaven and will forgive their sin and will heal their land (2 Chronicles 7:14).

Chapter 3   Beauty in Pregnancy: Not Mission Impossible

A definite benefit of being pregnant is the sudden appearance of a fine set of boobs. Buxom at last. However you enjoy your new-found figure, resist the temptation to chuck out your Wonderbras. We've all heard that beauty is fleeting; well this tends to be true when you're pregnant too. One day you've got a rosy complexion; the next you could give Barney the purple dinosaur a run for his money. One day your boobs are voluptuous and perky; the next they are just heavy and tender. On a positive note, the day that your tummy morphs into an obvious pregnant bump, you'll feel amazing.

Beauty is hard to put your finger on when you are changing from one day to the next. In the early weeks, if morning sickness is part of the picture, then simply surviving each day is the only focus. If you're lucky enough to emerge from this cloud at around 12–15 weeks, life can improve considerably. Pregnancy then continues as a kind of roundabout of enjoying your pregnant shape one day, then feeling like a bloater the next. So, a whole chapter dedicated to beauty in pregnancy? Well maybe it's because I'm a closet beauty-products freak, or maybe it's because there is something about a pregnant woman that reflects the beauty of the creator God in an intriguingly awesome way. Or maybe it's because I'm sitting here squeezing my ever-growing pregnant bump behind the laptop, grasping at straws that I will ever have anything vaguely resembling a flat stomach again.

Breasts

As I've already mentioned, a definite bonus in the beauty stakes is your blossoming bosom. Even if you never needed to before, get fitted for a proper bra that firmly cradles those tender breasts. You'll be relying on those ligaments to be supportive after the birth.

Hair and skin

Your hair should also look glossier than before, which if you're lucky can be matched with clearer skin. One of my friends actually realised that she must be pregnant by how translucent her skin suddenly became.

The all-over effect of pregnancy on your body is far-reaching. Pregnancy gives you a squeeze in every inch of your body, from hair to shoe size. It's a nine-month hug, as overwhelming as a hug from a bearded auntie with a penchant for lavender perfume. After its squeeze your body will take quite a while to return to "normal" if indeed it ever quite manages it.

What to wear

Unless you favour the baggy-skateboard look, your current wardrobe will be redundant sooner than you think. Before you know it, you'll be accosted by the growing niche market for maternity wear. You'll find a rollerblading model sporting a neat pregnant bump and fluffy poodle in most fashion catalogues. Looking in the high street? Hunt for the department that caters for petite, tall, large, extra large, extra-extra large. Just scoot on by past the *plus sizes* and you'll find the rack of garments with real girth – Maternity. If you detect a hint of weariness at maternity fashion, bear with me. At five feet tall and 34 weeks pregnant I am sure that I am wider than I am tall; I've not seen my knees for quite a while. Taut models sporting "bump", cute crop top and rollerblades do nothing to lift my spirits. Neither in fact does positioning the maternity fashion as part of the "outsize" department, next to the racks of truly awful shapeless leggings. I'd like to think I'm a switched-on smart consumer rather than a griping, hormone-overloaded woman, although my husband does wonder.

Alternatively, pilfering your husband's wardrobe can be quite fun. Enough to cheer up even the most progesterone-overloaded girls. The sporty look is flattering in the early months, certainly worth trying. Unfortunately my husband pulled rank on his sports attire and my pregnancy wardrobe went downhill rapidly.

What's your style?

Have you ever noticed that women in a group sometimes share a similar style? It's as if there's an unwritten rule that says, "We tend to wear fashion styles here", or another office/church/toddler group may be full of women for whom the unwritten rule is quite the opposite. Of course, we all tend to think that we would never consider dressing to fit in with a group, and we don't really care about how other people are dressing. Whether you care or not, being pregnant will certainly make you much more aware of how you look. I changed my usual style a bit when I was pregnant (I wasn't left much choice when he jammed his wardrobe shut every morning). However, it began to feel good to be stepping out of my usual clothing comfort zone, and breaking the mould a bit. Even the glossy pregnancy fashion pages were handy for a bit of inspiration. Let's not forget that God-given freedom and creativity is something to be enjoyed. Money and shape allowing, I'd encourage you to experiment with your style over the coming months. You are totally beautiful, and as you grow more and more pregnant you will reflect more and more of God's creative beauty. Pamper yourself – you're worth it!

> I bathed you with water and washed the blood from you and put ointments on you. I clothed you with an embroidered dress and put leather sandals on you. I dressed you in fine linen and covered you in costly garments... and a beautiful crown on your head... You became very beautiful and rose to be a queen (Ezekiel 16:9,10,12,13).

Exercise

It seems to me that pregnant women fall into two categories when it comes to exercise:

1. Those who do some exercise

My logic was that looking after a toddler all day is the equivalent of doing a half-marathon carrying a cannon ball. So, I remember putting myself smugly in the "I exercise regularly" category in my maternity notes. With hindsight, I think even swimming a few times a week might have prepared me for the big momma of physical exercise – giving birth.

Incidentally, somewhere along the line a midwife/doctor might casually ask you, "So, then, are you keeping up with your pelvic floor exercises?" My friend Ailsa mumbled something about her lounge floor being a bit too uneven and slippery, then went home and looked up "pelvic floor" in the dictionary to find out what it actually was. She was amazed to discover it concerned a whole set of muscles she never knew she had (even teachers don't know everything). The noteworthy point about pelvic floor exercises is this – doing them now will seriously improve your future sex life. Definitely a reason to rummage at the bottom of your bag for the pelvic floor leaflet you meant to read.

2. Those who enjoyed exercise as a big part of their lives before they got pregnant and continue throughout pregnancy

There are no two ways about it: exercise is a healthy part of normal pregnancy. Just whizz your proposed exercise plan past your midwife first. A good rule of thumb is only to exercise to the level at which you can still talk while you exercise. Obviously, you should avoid contact sports and becoming overheated. The benefits of remaining fit while pregnant are many, including finding a welcome relief from stress and a good way to maintain some stamina. The key is to remember that your body is entirely different from before. While exercising correctly during pregnancy has huge benefits, you must choose your sport and level of activity carefully. Your midwife will give you sound advice on this one.

Those who enjoyed lots of vigorous exercise may find it frustrating to ease off the pedal for nine months. It's certainly a tough call, loosening your grip slightly on other priorities and routines when you're pregnant. But surely, something as amazing as growing a baby is worth a bit of sacrifice and moderation. (Just don't forget those pelvic floor exercises and there'll be light at the end of the tunnel!)

Raw beauty and how to get it

When I was five, I was in a fancy-dress competition as a character called Zebedee. I was convinced that I'd win as I bounced around the school hall. Unfortunately, the coveted tub of sweets was not to be mine; the prize went to the girl dressed as a princess. For the first time, I compared my looks with that of someone else and wished that I looked better. It was a similar feeling to how I felt yesterday when my maternity trousers kept rolling down my bump in a room full of businesswomen in fitted suits. To be honest, the concept of being a beautiful woman in God's kingdom has just felt out of my grasp for a long time.

Until, that is, I spoke to a friend of mine, a mature Christian woman who just exudes the beauty of Jesus. When I first met her I was totally intrigued by the beauty that she had. True, she was fashionable and made a real effort to look good. But it was something much more than that. She didn't talk about God all the time but you could really tell that she was passionately in love with him. I suspected that it was her relationship with God that was at the root of her self-esteem and beauty. This intrigued me even more, because I hadn't really found much in the Bible about beauty. Paul's words about being modest have had a bad press, and most people assume that God's down on making the best of yourself. So one sunny afternoon I took my friend to task on this one. I wanted some answers on how she found out the nuts and bolts of being beautiful; the true beauty that only comes from heaven itself. So, over a couple of hot dogs, she told me about a woman whose story is told in the Bible. Her story is told in as much detail as all the men's stories put together...

Passion, unfaithfulness and intrigue

The Old Testament has been described as the longest, most passionate love affair ever recorded; it's the story of God and his people (his bride). Her story begins in Genesis and continues throughout the Bible. Today we call her "the church". The turbulent relationship documented between God and his people in the early days has an awesome foundation. This is that God was, and is, unswerving in his passion towards his bride. He pursued her and he longed for her. Their relationship began as God and the very first people walked together in the cool of the evening back in the Garden of Eden. Since then, kingdoms have risen and fallen, wars have been won and lost. The Old Testament records laughter, tears, rebellion, tender devotion, bravery, disobedience and obedience on the part of God's people. Through the chaos of Israel's history, there was one constant... the awesome devotion of God to his people.

> As a bridegroom rejoices over his bride, so will your God rejoice over you (Isaiah 62:5).

In his passionate love for his bride, the Father cherished, comforted and blessed his people. In times when they worshipped man-made images before him, he disciplined them. This was to be no three-way relationship, with his people dabbling in fake gods on the side. God was not compromising in his love; he called his people to do the same.

True passion

One of my favourite films of all time is *First Knight*, a thrilling romantic story starring Richard Gere. It is set in medieval

Camelot, where the people give their lives for Camelot and her queen. The city of Jerusalem arouses similar passion in today's world. Throughout history, and even now, men willingly fought and died for her. Jerusalem, as the home of God's people in the Old Testament, stirred the heart of the living God.

> See, I have engraved you on the palms of my hands; your walls are ever before me (Isaiah 49:16).

Despite this love, God's people rebelled, chased other idols and got caught in a cycle of good works and self-importance. The very reason that Jesus came was to clear the decks of all these sin barriers between God and his people. When Jesus hung on the cross and cried, "It is finished!", it was the shout of victory, signalling that nothing could ever again come between God and his people.

Eden beauty

Through Jesus' precious sacrifice, the love relationship that began in the cool of the day in Eden is ours to enjoy. This is the place to find your true beauty. This is where raw beauty is: walking in the cool of the evening with your God. Oh, how he longs for you!

Can you catch the vision? Real beauty rests in the truth that as God's child you are totally and utterly cherished and precious to him. He calls you beautiful. God calls me beautiful not for what I look like, or even for what good I might do. I am beautiful because I am his.

Sometimes (often), I find it quite hard to let these truths be reality in my day-to-day life. Why? Well I'm no expert, but I'd bet my mushroom korma that my own self-image sometimes gets in the way.

Self-image

Amazingly, by the age of five, our self-concept, the person we think we are in relation to others, is so firmly established that we will resist efforts to change it. From then on the attitude of family and other life experiences mould what kind of person we think we are. No wonder then that some women ease into pregnancy naturally and some of us feel like a duck out of water in the maternal stakes. Stripped of our previous shape, fitness level and daytime role, even the most maternal of us need the occasional self-image "DIY SOS".

One blistering August afternoon, when I was eight months pregnant with my first baby, I decided to walk to my friend's house, a couple of miles away. Mobile phone, maternity notes and energy sweets in bag (labour wasn't going to catch *me* out), off I skipped down the road (I lie: read "waddled"). Well, by the time I arrived I probably resembled a puffing water buffalo on heat. Now this friend of mine, Martine, welcomed me into her home. She took my shoes off and ran a bath for me, adding her best aromatherapy oils, and she lit the bathroom with candles. Fresh, fluffy towels and a magazine were next to the bath. I had no idea she had planned this for me. It was particularly nice as we didn't have a bath in our tiny flat (just a shower). I stayed in that bath for hours. Still to this day that afternoon goes down as one of my best five afternoons ever. So I urge you to give yourself a break this pregnancy, too.

Self-image reality check

Even if you've got a house full of carpet-biting children, or you're forever chasing your tail at work, take a self-image reality check. The raw truth is you are more beautiful in God's sight than you can begin to imagine. You haven't got to strive all the time. It is not a waste of time to step back and assess what you're doing and where you're going with everything. Take it easy this pregnancy – you and your baby are worth it. Incidentally, steer clear of a drastic hair cut as a treat. I tried it when I was heavily pregnant and ended up looking like a rotund hedgehog, but that's another story.

Time out with your Father God

Think back to the day when you first met Jesus. Got it? Now imagine that you are walking in the cool of the evening, talking together. It's such a beautiful evening. Then he reaches out and gives you a present. It's a huge white lily, and it has a label with the words:

> Therefore, if anyone is in Christ, he is a new creation; the old has gone, the new has come! (2 Corinthians 5:17).

You are a new, fresh person in him. Even your self-image can change. Indeed it is a colossal tragedy if we don't allow God to heal and shape our self-image. This is what our new beauty and self-image can now rest upon:

1. A sense of family (your Father God is the most faithful that there is. He is preparing a place for you in heaven).
2. A sense of value (Jesus thinks you're precious enough to die for).
3. A sense of hope (the future is bright when God is on your side).

It is the very beauty of Jesus within you that will open the eyes of your child to his Creator God.

Mother...[is] all-enveloping, protective, nourishing... Mother is food; she is love; she is warmth; she is earth. To be loved by her means to be alive, to be rooted, to be at home.

(Erich Fromm 1900–1980)

Chapter 4   What If...?

My "hot tip" for pregnancy has got to be that it is worth having at least one outfit that you feel really good in. At least then you'll avoid the misery of being the only one at the party wearing the same outfit that you weeded the garden in the day before. I'm no slim chick at the best of times, so by 20 weeks pregnant I already had plenty of worries about what I would look like in a few more months' time. As if visions of looking like a waterlogged slug weren't bad enough, take a peek at the rest of my worries...

Pregnancy worries

- My whole life is going to change. It feels as if things are spinning out of control!
- My emotions are all over the place; what's going on?
- Am I "bonding" with the baby?
- Am I still attractive?
- I feel really sick if I don't eat korma. It's driving me crazy.
- What if something goes wrong?

Since I wrote this list, I have chatted with many women in the throes of pregnancy and discovered that we often share the same worries. Hence, this chapter is dedicated to taking a look at them. For what it's worth, I'm no psychology expert or eminent theologian on the subject of worries. Actually, I'm a class-one worrier myself, and I'm even worse under the influence of pregnancy hormones. However, I'm starting to walk in the faithfulness of God, and I'm clutching the Father's hand at each step of this pregnancy. If a panic situation does occur during your pregnancy, having a few encouragements under your belt might just come in handy. A top pregnancy worry, "sense of control", can take a beating from the early weeks of pregnancy, so let's look at that first.

Sense of control

Lots of us gain a fair amount of focus and a sense of purpose from our jobs. Many of us get satisfaction from a hobby, or from seeing friends. We know who our friends are, and how we fit in to our social circle. Sometimes, though, finding out that you are pregnant can have the effect of completely pulling the rug from under your feet in a number of ways. I remember worrying that I wouldn't be "one of the girls" any more. Maybe the thought of maternity leave has made you wonder how indispensable you really are at work. Pregnancy sickness is very common, and some of us feel so rough that we can hardly move, let alone enjoy meeting friends or indulging in a game of tennis. Any of these situations, coupled with a generous dose of pregnancy hormones, can leave any woman sobbing into her fortified milk wondering why it feels as if her life is spinning out of control. Where's my life going?

The excellent thing about this question, at any time of your life, is that it makes you lay your cards on the table. While all this change can be more than a little bit scary, at least it provides a chance to downshift from the rat race and reassess where your focus and purpose is really coming from.

Last summer I spoke to Viv, who took great pride in her job in accountancy. When she found out that she was pregnant she was absolutely thrilled, if not a little surprised. The baby wasn't planned, but was very much wanted. However, Viv couldn't get away from the fact that her life seemed to have changed beyond recognition overnight. For the first time, she felt like a real fish out of water. So she went shopping and bought a copy of every parenting book she could find. At her local Christian bookshop she subscribed to numerous parenting magazines, then bought up half of a baby shop on her way home. However, in her rush to increase her own confidence, she overlooked the only true resource of God himself.

Often it isn't until we realise how shallow are the things that we rely on, that we remember God. The world shouts at us to get self-esteem by being pleased with who we are. Actually, real self-confidence is being pleased with who God says we are.

Getting your self-esteem from heaven's stocks

Really "touching base" with getting your self-esteem from heaven's stocks, rather than your own, means letting go of some of your securities. This is the tricky bit, and it certainly feels risky. I saw a T-shirt once with a picture of a surfer, surfing without a board. The caption was "St Peter's School of Surf". Peter had to take that leap of faith onto the water, trusting Jesus with his life. Yet what a place to be when he finally took that leap!

> "Lord, if it's you," Peter replied, "tell me to come to you on the water."
>
> "Come," he said.
>
> Then Peter got down out of the boat, walked on the water and came towards Jesus (Matthew 14:28,29).

I think that God has given us pregnant women a helping hand when it comes to letting go and gaining our confidence and sense of purpose from him. What could that be? Our hormones! Let me introduce hormones, our friends rather than our enemies.

The potential of hormones

Hormones are chemical messengers produced by one part of the body (such as the ovaries, or the placenta during pregnancy) and then released into the bloodstream where they travel to another area to produce a particular effect. Once you're pregnant, your body's hormone levels undergo superfast changes. The level of progesterone rises to ten times its level before conception, while the amount of oestrogen produced in a single day is equivalent to what a non-pregnant woman would produce in three years. Not bad! Like it or not, your hormones play a vital role in preparing and maintaining your body for pregnancy and birth. During the first few months you may not look pregnant, but the effects of hormones will soon ensure that you feel pregnant (oh yes, indeed). High levels of oestrogen, progesterone and human chorionic gonadotrophin (HCG) can affect you in many different ways. For example, needing to pee more often occurs because higher progesterone levels result in the relaxation of the bladder muscles. Pregnancy hormones get a bad press because they are responsible for all those niggling symptoms that show that your body is adapting for motherhood.

Hormones intensify our maternal focus as they increase our zoom on our baby, and decrease our zoom on the rest of the world. I think this is one of the reasons that God designed hormones. I also think that God created hormones to help us become soft-hearted and open to his touch at such a crucial time in our life. It is only when we soften our hearts before

God that we can draw on his strength rather than on our own shallow resources.

The strength of a woman

Having roller-coaster emotions has got to be one of the most bewildering parts of pregnancy. Indeed, crying into the sofa after an episode of *Big Brother* is not uncommon. Suddenly becoming more sensitive can take a bit of getting used to. However, this really does not need to be on any pregnant woman's list of worries. The plain truth is that a more sensitive heart is a brilliant preparation for both motherhood and a better walk with God. New mums, with soft hearts, reflect the responsiveness of Jesus to the Father in a completely unique way. Just one sight of the Father's face, filled with love, draws Jesus at once to respond. The woman in the Song of Songs revelled in the love of her king. Her words show how we are to respond to Jesus, our "lover".

> Listen! My lover! Look! Here he comes, leaping across the mountains, bounding over the hills. My lover is like a gazelle or a young stag. Look! There he stands behind our wall, gazing through the windows, peering through the lattice. My lover spoke and said to me, "Arise my darling, my beautiful one, and come with me" (Song of Songs 2:8–10).

The true strength of a woman lies in her responsiveness to the Father. If we are truly open to the Holy Spirit, we become stronger than we could ever imagine. We are called to stand in the gap for our husbands and children; nobody else can fill this position. If we soften our hearts and take up this challenge, our walk with God will become a thrilling adventure and our families will be blessed.

Bonding with the baby

After discussing the worries of lack of self-confidence and roller-coaster emotions, let's look at a less well discussed worry, about bonding with the baby. A good friend of mine, Rebecca, is currently 19 weeks pregnant with her first baby. Since she became pregnant, I've really noticed how she trusts God rather than flying into a panic (as I have a tendency to do!). We were chatting on the phone the other week and she commented that she was a bit worried that she didn't feel amazingly close to her baby. The standard response usually given by doctors/midwives/mothers-in-law in this situation is "Don't worry about it. Lots of women don't feel a rush of love at first. For some it develops over time". Rebecca is a midwife, so she already knows this advice like the back of her hand. There is certainly nothing wrong with it. Yet Rebecca has since mentioned that she believes that God wants to release her from this particular worry, and save her the misery of fretting about bonding all through her pregnancy. The Bible already tells us that God has a unique destiny for each new creation. So, her thinking was that maybe she would join in and start praying as the Father is shaping her baby. The last time I spoke to her, she said that praying about her baby's future has made "bonding" take on a whole new dimension.

Prayer is not a one-way conversation

I discovered something similar for myself when I was pregnant with Samuel (now aged two, and passionate about rockets). I started to find that the "Please God, protect my baby" prayer was a bit impersonal. I wanted to see my baby as Jesus saw him, so I could love him and pray for him on a deeper level. A week later, I was lying in a bed in my local maternity hospital. As I had had severe pre-eclampsia in my previous pregnancy, I was being monitored very closely this time round. My blood pressure kept shooting up and I spent so long in the maternity ward that I knew what days they served mashed potato, and how to trick the drinks machine into dishing out hot chocolate. Anyway, one night I was beside myself with worry about this baby, as I had been admitted to hospital again. I was missing my little one at home (and his dad) like crazy.

I spotted a Bible in the hospital locker, and I read some words that really touched me:

> You will make them [your sons] princes throughout the land (Psalm 45:16, brackets mine).

The awesome privilege of having a baby really hit home, so I started to pray words of hope and destiny for my little one, rather than fretting about him. I suppose I'm finally learning that prayer wasn't meant to be a one-way conversation. Praying for my baby in this way was like being allowed a peek through the keyhole of heaven's door. Surely there can be no better way to begin to bond with your child.

Relationship worries

Everybody would like family relationships that really work; every women's magazine you pick up has relationship tips. Being pregnant certainly seems to make most women look at relationships in the home in a different light. The marriage partnership gets a good deal of attention in the Christian world. It must be said, however, that there are a number of things about being married and pregnant that they don't tell you at church. One pregnancy worry that is hardly ever discussed in Christian circles is "What if I'm not as attractive to my husband any more?" Even as early as eight weeks into your pregnancy you may have noticed that sometimes you feel ravishing and other times you feel as alluring as the aforementioned waterlogged slug. While all the books tell you that your husband will find your changing shape really attractive, it's sometimes hard to feel all floaty and feminine when your spend half your waking hours feeling as sick as a dog. This seesaw is caused partly by your hormones, and won't last forever. Try and resist the temptation to slob around the house wearing baggy leggings, saggy jumpers and an attitude to match. To your husband you are a beacon of femininity, and changing lusciously. Make the most of it! Actually, lots of women say that it was only when pregnant, with all their barriers down, that they really enjoyed their whole marriage relationship. No contraception – yippee! Just yesterday I talked to a new mum about this and she said she wished that she had enjoyed those long, lazy lie-ins with her husband while she had the chance. Wistfully, she concluded, "Sex? I remember that..."

Tensions about who now does what around the house can also exaggerate any worries you have about changing roles. Having a baby can be the start of the slippery slope to becoming a nagging wife. Don't let it happen! Sort things out sooner, rather than later. Parenting can pull the rug from under you if you haven't already laid the foundation of respecting each other, despite any failings.

Eating for three

You (and your husband) may have already noticed that your stomach and breasts have swollen slightly. While your husband may be thrilled that you are "showing", you know that the likelihood is that your swollen tummy is actually due to the family pack of Mars bars that you ate last night. Hence the worry we probably all share about how much/what we are eating. Madonna was pregnant at the same time that I was with Joseph. No doubt she craved only boiled cabbage, because she slipped back into her hipsters days after giving birth. Meanwhile, I was left sobbing at the sight of my jelly tummy and regretting every multipack of cheese sticks that I ever consumed. My problem was that from about week seven, I had two options: either I felt really sick, or I ate cheese sticks and felt slightly better. I went for option B.

It is amazing how appetites and tastes change during much of pregnancy. Normal enjoyment of food often goes out of the window and it's easy to end up feeling really fed up and guilty for not being in the happy club. Where you can, I'd pamper yourself with luxurious long baths, or curl up in front of a good comedy film. Many women find that nibbling dry toast or food containing ginger helps slightly. My friend swore by ice lollies, as at least a reasonable distraction to her nine-month quagmire of nausea. I suppose it beats gnawing on coal.

What if...

Pregnancy is certainly not easy when you find yourself worrying "What if something goes wrong?" This is the worry that pounces on you if you have a tummy ache, a slight bleed, or someone on *Friends* has a miscarriage. Miscarrying is the biggest worry of all, even though thousands of women have a bleed at some time during their pregnancy and the pregnancy still continues successfully. Nevertheless, any bleeding during pregnancy should always be reported to a doctor.

I remember one freezing January night when, as I packed away the Christmas decorations, I was talking to God as if he were right next to me. I really sensed the security of being his child and that I could really be free and not worry about things. I was eight weeks pregnant, and I gave thanks from the bottom of my heart. After two years of trying to get pregnant, and undergoing infertility investigations, it was great to lift this little one up to him. The house was empty as the others were out, so I let rip and sang my heart out to him and had a bit of a boogie.

The next day I miscarried our little one. At first I felt that I was banging on heaven's door and no one was listening. I shouted in anger and desperation at God. A mother who had also known such pain once said, "It is the noise of your own tears that can stop you hearing the weeping of a Father who never intended his children to suffer such pain." I never thought it would happen to me. Yet, in the midst of my confusion, it was as if a pure white ribbon of God's peace touched my every emotion and every tear. During my time with God the night before, I had acknowledged God as the giver of life. I couldn't dictate when the life I held began or ended. I held on to the sovereignty of my God.

All the days ordained for me were written in your book before one of them came to be (Psalm 139:16).

In the face of my worst-case scenario...

Whether my little one's life lasted eight weeks, or 80 years, it was ordained by God and God cherished him. I believe I learned some real nuggets of truth from what we went through that bitter winter. I learned that children are a gift. I cannot control a gift; I cannot dictate when it will arrive or what it will be like; I can only receive it. I also learned that trusting in God is not a way of calling down a blanket ban on all unpleasant experiences. It's a fact that we live in a fallen world that is not running the way that God intended it to run because it has turned its back on its creator. Most of all, I learned that even in the face of my "worst-case scenario" my God didn't leave me for a moment. And I trust him more as the giver of life than I did before. I'd like you to know that there is no worry, fear or even reality that is greater than your God. The love of a mother for her baby is like a raindrop compared to the ocean of love that God has for that little one.

Remember this...

The vast majority of pregnancies are problem-free from start to finish. If things do start to go a bit off track, get good obstetric care and remember this: the God who made your little one is the God who flung stars into space, moved mountains and raised the dead. While I have known God as my comforter during times when I have faced loss, I have also experienced God doing the absolutely miraculous. So...

> God is our refuge and strength, an ever-present help in trouble. Therefore we will not fear, though the earth give way and the mountains fall into the heart of the sea, though its waters roar and foam... (Psalm 46:1–3).

Time out with your Father God

Is anything worrying you? Write down any worries in the space below. Now, take a different-coloured pen and write in bold letters on top of the worries:

Come to me, all you who are weary and burdened, and I will give you rest (Matthew 11:28).

Talk your worry out with your Father God. Enjoy your miracle.

Remember: if any symptom of your pregnancy is giving you concern, you must always inform your midwife or obstetrician without delay. Always keep your antenatal appointments.

Chapter 5   Maybe It's Time We
Got a Scalextric...

Last week my husband and I braved the shopping mall with
our menagerie of sticky shoplifters. Diving for a lift with a
double toddler buggy and a pregnant bump is never easy, and
we were just about to resort to humping the cherubs up the
stairs, dangling buggy over shoulder, when a strangely familiar "Hey, Funsize..." stopped me in my tracks. "Funsize" was
my nickname at university – I like to think it was because I
was full of energy and sweet, like a funsize Mars bar. (Not
because I'm short and olive-skinned.) Anyway, by the lift were
a couple of university friends who had got engaged at the
same time as we did. There they were, looking grown up (does
that mean *we're* supposed to have grown up?) and, yes, most
definitely pregnant. Only you couldn't tell which one. Both
man and wife were sporting a pert pregnant bump. It tran-
spired that he was actually wearing an "empathy belly", a
foam-filled lump that a man can strap around his waist, to
give him a "real experience of what it's like to be pregnant".
Exchanging pleasantries, we found out that they had "their"
water birth booked for next month in the company of their
antenatal instructor, who had so kindly lent them the empathy belly. They talked, animated, about what promised to be
the ultimate birth experience, a true touchy-feely whirligig of
pleasure. Wistful, I glanced down at my cherubs in the buggy.
Joseph was breathing on a glass-fronted biscuit counter then

licking it off, and Samuel had his willy out and was stretching it to see how far it would go. Twang! Time to move on...

"All the best, then."

"We'll have to meet up some time."

Off they waddled to the lift. My husband couldn't wipe the look of disbelief off his face. I wiped the smears from the biscuit counter and swooned, "How sweet to actually want to know what it feels like to be pregnant. Did you see he even had a birth magazine in his rucksack? Birth should be a two-way experience... What a sweetie, don't you think?"

My husband's bemused reply: "He used to be a decent guy..."

Herein lies the difference between men and women regarding the whole pregnancy experience.

Pregnancy-tinted glasses

To a woman, every bit of pregnancy from stretch marks to pram choice is a big deal. Every detail matters to her, and every emotion is felt in true Technicolor. Any previous feminist tendencies are temporarily put on hold as she absolutely expects to be treated with the utmost care and given full attention during this monumental time. After all, she is *pregnant*. Everything is seen through pregnancy-tinted glasses.

For most men, all the same emotional ingredients are there: euphoria, panic, excitement, fear. However, rather than teasing every inch out of each emotion, like a woman, they see this emotion cocktail as a pouncing tiger to be avoided whenever possible. Or, at least, kept in its place.

The classic male approach to pregnancy

As far as the slightly mystifying physical aspects are concerned, the classic male approach tends to be:

One of awe (at the sheer size of your breasts) combined with fear (Have you SEEN the film *Aliens*?) combined with moderate/extreme concern (for your well-being, of course, not for whether he'll ever have sex again). Ultimately, the classic male handle on it all is to see pregnancy as a process, a means to an end. Most days he manages the bizarre combination of being both nervous and complacent.

This weird combination is not thinly disguised male bravado. It's due to two realities.

Firstly, all this change makes most men nervous. What if you are never again the person they married? Are you going to be OK? What if you turn into your mother? They don't want to lose you.

Secondly, "empathy belly" aside, I think that someone who has never been pregnant can't ever truly get into your shoes and completely understand what it is really like. He can imagine, but only in the way that we can imagine what it must feel like if he gets hit in his most sensitive spot by a football. Remember the mantra "pregnancy is a process, a means to an end" and you won't go far wrong on your man's psyche. Men don't wear pregnancy-tinted glasses 24/7. While their eyes are on the end in sight, our eyes are on the here and now. That's why the day-to-day niggles of pregnancy don't mean the same to them as they do to us. This difference can be the source of huge frustration on the part of the woman. The answer? Well, I've not personally got this one nailed yet, but here are a few nuggets that have served me well this pregnancy.

A couple of nuggets of wisdom

1) I try not to get him to wear my pregnancy-tinted glasses all the time. I am beginning to accept that he will approach pregnancy differently from me, and maybe I shouldn't be trying to force him to do it my way all the time. The more I hassle him to approach the pregnancy my way, the less confident he feels in his own abilities. He's a daddy-to-be. I'm going to give him a break.

2) I try to avoid these common sentence-starters:
   "I know you're not really interested, but..."
   "I hope you're not going to do that when we've got a baby."
   "I'm the one going through this, you know."
   "You've got no idea what I'm going through."
   These sentences are enough to make anyone's self-esteem crash and burn. Just imagine what would result if we built him up instead, and communicated our needs in a way that wasn't so hard on him.

You might have guessed that this chapter is not one to surreptitiously leave open on the coffee table hoping that he'll pick it up and finally be enlightened as to what it's really like to be you. This chapter is a peek into the world of a daddy-to-be.

Nose architecture

Nose architecture is the last thing you would think a new mum would be thinking about as she gazes at her sleeping newborn. Not that my baby had a big nose, not pointy, not bulbous or crooked, and definitely not hooked. Just a standard-issue baby button nose. (Very slightly ski-jumped.) Well, I had two problems with it.

Firstly, I no doubt started life with the very same button nose (slightly ski-jump). However, it morphed during childhood into a fully contoured ski-jump nose. I'm not talking slightly upturned, I'm talking a curve so convex that you could ski a triple flip off it. That was my problem: I just knew that my baby's innocent little button nose would turn on him and go ski-jump; I just knew it.

Secondly, my understanding of genes is that you get dominant and recessive. In the great battle of the genes, the dominant always wins; that's what I got taught by buxom Mrs Bleloch in the biology department. So, Mrs Bleloch in your retirement apartment in Florida, enlighten me. My husband has classic French bone structure. Strong in every way, square jaw, prominent cheekbones, straight nose. So why do our offspring end up with my runty little nose that bucks all laws of nature?

Let's face it, the subject of genes usually belongs in biology classes and Channel Four documentaries. When your offspring come along, it almost becomes interesting, discussing (arguing over) who gave what gene. While I'd like to claim that I donated the walk-early gene I've a sneaking suspicion that I actually originated the "always-spill-food-down-my-top" gene that my boys have faithfully continued. For the daddies-to-be, passing on their characteristics gets a definite thumbs-up.

I was really pleased when we found out that Sue was pregnant, we've wanted this for a long time. It seems like a long way off though! It feels good to be packaging up my genes for the future. (Hopefully he or she will have my good ones.)

(Andy, 32)

Daddy-to-be

I picked up a pregnancy magazine last week and realised something quite outrageous that I'd never really noticed before. There was barely a page that did not allude somewhere to the man's "ten-minute contribution" to the pregnancy (i.e. conception). The general tone, while tongue-in-cheek, was that it was self-indulgence on their part, and lucky for them that something "of essence" had resulted (the baby). OK, the woman does have a tremendous physical, emotional and spiritual journey to make. But surely becoming a father is more than donating a few genes...

I'm going to be a dad!

Is the fathering of a baby not worthy of note any more? I honestly hadn't thought of it like this until I flicked through that magazine. It's so common to hear pregnant women having a giggle about how he "did his bit" nine months ago. I'm not nitpicking here; girly banter is my thing. However, maybe we have lost the plot a little in our generation, as to the significance of fathering a baby. Maybe we miss the point.

Fathering a baby is a gift from God, just as becoming a mother is. God alone initiates the call upon the man's life to be a father, and for this reason he is worthy of honour from those around him. Imagine the sense of honour Moses must have felt as God said, "I will make your descendants as numerous as the stars" (Exodus 32:13). God was giving Moses an awesome gift: fatherhood. Becoming a father represented hope and a future for the people. Time and time again, I've skipped over the "so-and-so begat so-and-so, so-and-so begat so-and-so" lists scattered through the Old Testament. Why were such meticulous paternity lists included in God's word?

Maybe because fatherhood is something to be recognised and honoured.

An expectant dad's first reactions to impending parenthood usually include a secret smug smile to himself that he "scored the golden goal". A sense of exhilaration, even if it is accompanied by panic. Christian men often feel re-energised in the might of God upon the news of pregnancy. If God can do this, he can do anything. Some men feel a new sense of purpose in life, others take it upon themselves to reorganise the family finances, or suddenly want to sit down for meals together instead of in front of the television. Others may simply be silently reassessing their priorities. It may not be obvious to others, but the news of impending fatherhood has an impact deep down. There is a sense of pride. What initiated the stirring deep inside? The God-given sense of honour that accompanies fatherhood.

I have a confession to make...

I'm afraid I have thrown a "pregnancy tantrum" because my husband wouldn't get me frankfurters from the minimarket at midnight. I've even pounced on him to build the crib RIGHT NOW as he walked in from work, even though he'd had a long day and wanted a shower. Who was the pregnant wife who spent money on baby clothes when I knew he needed the money for petrol? It was me! OK, so progesterone does funny things to me, but even so...

Here's a thought that I just can't get out of my head...

HIS FRAGILE SENSE OF HONOUR AT BECOMING A FATHER COULD QUITE EASILY BE SMOTHERED BY A PREGNANT WIFE WHO DEMANDS SOMETHING AKIN TO SUBSERVIENCE TO HER, THE PREGNANT ONE.

That thought makes me cry.

Dare we lose respect for our men purely because we're the pregnant ones? Do we act as if we are the only ones that matter in the household? Are we smothering his honour with our self-centredness?

A new generation of pioneers

Throughout history, men have led their families forward into new territory; they have fought for their tribes, sailed the sea to undiscovered lands, and ridden across prairies, deserts and jungles in the search of better things for their families. What about our generation? Is a man's lot these days just about grinding out 9–5 in a job and keeping the wife happy? Do the images of the brave adventurers belong only in the latest Hollywood blockbuster? Do stories of pioneers belong only in the dusty pages of *Little House on the Prairie*?

Well, stoke up your sardine smoothie, because you and your husband may be in for a nice surprise...

Prairie man

Imagine, for a moment, your husband sitting on a fine stallion. His head is held high as he surveys the prairies for the perfect piece of land. He is clutching with white knuckles a huge stake with a flag tied onto it. The flag bears your family surname; it flaps noisily in the wind. Imagine his face, full of honour, his eyes focused on the task ahead. A tap of his foot and the horse obeys without question. He is racing across the plains to claim the land for his family. In the distance he stops, and without hesitation he lifts the stake high then plunges it triumphantly into the ground he has claimed for his family. This is an analogy of a first-time father leading his new family into the unknown territory of parenthood.

He has honour because he is to be a dad.
He is brave because he knows God is with him.
He has vision because God has given him hope.
He can do it because his wife is at his side.

Tough choices

Many years ago a young man, Caleb, was at a similar cross-
roads in his life. God was showing Moses, Caleb, Joshua and
other men the "promised land", the new territory chosen by
God to be a blessing to his people. Caleb had a choice to make.
He had to decide whether to remain in the wilderness, which
might have been rough, directionless and unsatisfying but at
least was familiar, or to go on an expedition to discover the
incredible inheritance that God had in store for him. Doubts
about leaving the familiarity of the wilderness and heading
into unknown territory must have been very real. He had no
previous experience of the area, no maps and no army, but he
knew God was with him. Caleb made his choice: "We can certainly do it" (Numbers 13:30).

God's plan was to bring millions of his people into their
promised land, a land of hope for the future. God's plan for
fatherhood is just the same. At this crucial stage in family life
he calls every mum and dad to step out and discover the life
he has for you. What promised land does he intend for *you*?
What familiar wilderness is he asking you to leave behind?

What could stop a man reaching his potential as a new dad?

Let's rewind to the image of your man on horseback, ready to
race into the promised land and stake his claim for your family. Is there anything distracting him from setting off on his

journey? In other words... are there any ropes lying around the horse's hooves that could trip it up?

Here are a few of the common ones...

Rope around the hoof number one: money worries

I know babies cost money; my friends with kids are always broke.

(Geoff, 25)

The pressure of having to earn enough money is a knot in the stomach for a lot of dads-to-be. I suspect that even our friend "empathy man" had occasional twinges of panic about this one. There is no getting away from the fact that babies cost money, and your family income may well be decreasing at the same time as a baby comes along. A double whammy with the force of a sledgehammer: quite enough momentum to send any man hotfooting it to the computer store for some "head in the sand" relief.

A few years ago I worked in the local mother-and-baby superstore. That was when I picked up the vibe that money is one big sensitive issue during pregnancy. Picture this. A newly pregnant couple meandering light-headedly through the store, hungrily taking it all in. Eyeing up the other parents-to-be, clearly recognisable by their matching glee. More often than not, the woman is casually popping a few items in an oversized basket. A cot mobile with programmable songs, a cute little traditional teddy, a couple of embroidered blankets, a couple of bras. Just a few essentials. They exchange warm glances as they wait in the queue at the checkout; they could get used to this. The total flashes up in green neon, and the man does a double take. "...*HOW* MUCH????"

They walk to the car in silence. She interprets his reluctance to part with the cash as a sign that he is mean, and that he isn't thinking of her and the baby's needs. He interprets her face of thunder as a sign that she is taking for granted how hard he is working for the family. Sticky patch number one. This one is so common that every new mum I mentioned it to rolled her eyes at the memory. Between cheese paninis and wine, these new mums and I (the forever pregnant one) cobbled together some solutions to the whole "HOW MUCH?" issue. These ideas may not be rocket science, but they might just help you ease that "money rope" from around your horse's foot.

Possible solution

1) LOOK at the actual prices of essentials in a range of mother-and-baby stores.
2) Work out TOGETHER how much you can afford to spend without going into debt. Debt is never worth it.
3) This is the best bit: GO SHOPPING with your list and KEEP WITHIN YOUR BUDGET.

In a crazy way I was secretly pleased that my husband had suddenly turned into Mr Thrifty. At least one of us was taking the responsibility of feeding more mouths seriously. For a few moments there I felt like a grown up!

4) Resist the urge to act like a spoilt child when you see the baby furniture of your dreams. Yes it's on offer, yes it's utterly perfect, yes you get free accessories. However, there is nothing more humiliating for a man than to have his wife throwing such a wobbly in a baby store that he is

forced to give in sheepishly as the assistants titter behind the baby baths.

5) LOOK AT YOUR LIFESTYLE. A friend of mine swears by a money diary. She writes down everything that she spends each day. She says that she's now much more aware of where her money is going, and that has made her feel more in control of her finances.

Rope around the foot number two: the fear that the woman he married has gone forever

Imagine you're a dad-to-be, a happy chap. One day your previously stable wife morphs into a sobbing, ravenous individual who spends her evenings on Internet birth sites and won't trust takeaways any more. She waits to pounce on you with baby-name books or a baby nest that needs building as soon as you get in from work. And there's more. Her breasts swell to a luscious size, and you're barely allowed a glimpse. What's going on?

Our dad-to-be secretly worries if this is normal. Pregnancy is not supposed to be an audition for "Victim of the brain snatchers". What's going on?

Possible solution

If you find yourself with a moment to spare between scrubbing the light switches and whipping up some gherkin ice cream, try just sitting down next to your man. Then try talking about how pregnancy is affecting you both. Hear each other out. This is not the time to bring up past grievances or throw in your birth-plan ideas. Most of all, REASSURE HIM THAT YOU ARE STILL YOU. Now here's a treat for you both that is definitely worth a try. Light a candle or two, snuggle up and don't talk about babies for a whole evening. He just might have been missing you like mad... He won't be able to venture into new things if you're not united any more.

Some couples renew their wedding vows to each other when they reach a significant milestone, such as 25 years. Why wait till then? What could be a more significant milestone than starting a family? You could renew your vows in private, a special day shared together. Or you could invite friends and family round to share the milestone with you.

Rope around the foot number three: he will be unable to help his wife during labour

Our typical daddy-to-be might actually be more scared of labour than he will admit. Before you throw your arms up in indignation, I suspect that, if he is scared (far be it from me to presume), it is primarily because you are his treasure and he wants to protect you. The most common worries include fear of fainting, fear of blood, and a fear of losing you. He hates the thought of being thrown into a situation in which he has no real idea of who's in charge and what's going to happen next. He is sure he will be out of his depth, and he is not comfortable with that thought.

Possible solution number 1

Avoid the hospital stress machine entirely and opt for a home birth. I heartily recommend this option, as long as your pregnancy and health are free from medical complication. Many couples with trouble-free pregnancies have found that a home birth is an empowering, uniting experience. A planned home birth has nullified many a man's fears and allows the event to be anticipated rather than feared.

Possible solution number 2

Most of the men in my circle of friends are not keen on hospitals and do not relish the thought of even leaving the car park, let alone entering the inner sanctum of a maternity ward. OK, a few may be enticed by the promise that there will be gadgets and devices they can cast their eye over. My friend's partner, apparently, spent the whole of her labour transfixed by the contraction monitor. You can just imagine it...

> Her: Oh, this contraction really hurts. Oh, oh, oh, agggghoh, oh, oh aaaaggggh! That was the biggest one so far.
>
> Him: Erm, I think you'll find that actually the biggest one so far was the one at 1:26am.

For some guys, the contraptions and black plastic mattresses are like their worst nightmare, and do little to calm their sense of unease. For these men, a face-to-face meeting with the team in charge of your care might make the world of difference. An opportunity for you both to ask questions and raise any concerns is an almost guaranteed way of reducing anxiety. By the end of my first hospital appointment my husband was satisfied that the clinical standards were far better than the décor in the waiting room would suggest. I was "systems go" as far as he was concerned. Minutes later, I lost the car keys in the ladies' toilet, but that's another story. Nevertheless, as my pregnancy progressed he became much more accustomed to hospitals and medical talk; by the end he was actually quite jovial with my obstetrician.

Possible solution number 3

Another solution you may want to discuss is having a "birth partner" with you during labour. A birth partner can be a friend of yours, or in some areas you can hire experienced birth partners or "doulas". In the UK the midwife's primary role is to support the woman in labour, emotionally as well as physically. The word midwife actually means "with woman". You should find that her support is more than adequate. Getting the support you need over this time may well ease the anxiety for both of you, and may result in him chilling out over the whole thing.

Popular in Holland and other European countries, a "doula" can be hired to support you in labour. Independent midwives operate worldwide and can provide much of the care in your own home. Studies have shown that a woman in labour who feels she is being emotionally supported has less fear and anxiety. Less fear and anxiety means that the labour is usually easier. So maybe having extra support could give more advantages than you realised!

Rope around the foot number four: feeling trapped and full of doubt

> *I couldn't stop thinking that my life was over now that we were having a baby. We had planned it, but it started feeling like the pregnancy wasn't my choice. I felt trapped and maybe a bit resentful of my delighted wife.*

If we were all really honest, I think both men and women would admit that they have doubts and fears during pregnancy that they would rather not admit to. Doubts about the timing of having a baby, doubts about the strength of the marriage and doubts about parenting ability are the common ones. Throw in a generous dose of guilt for having such thoughts, and ZAP, you find yourself feeling trapped.

For a man, doubt is a particularly lonely zone. Unless he has a close friend he can talk to, doubts tend to be bottled up deep inside. For many a man, the doubt about whether he'll make a good dad is one that is hard to shake off. If he grew up in a happy family, he might feel inadequate as he compares himself to his own father. If he grew up with a father figure who was less than ideal, his image of what makes a good dad might come from TV, friends, his pastor or a combination of influences. Either way, worries about making the grade as a father abound.

Possible solution
The first step is to be honest with each other about any doubts or misgivings about the pregnancy. Doubt is fed by loneliness, and gathers momentum as it whirls around your head. It can be such a relief to share the "I don't know if I can do this" worry with the one person who understands you the best (and may well have similar worries!).

Secondly, this is the time to hook up with other new parents (if you haven't already). Get to know people who have had a baby and survived the first year of "babydom". Yes, they still have a life (most of the time). Yes, they still enjoy a party! Yes, they are more exhausted than they ever thought possible, but they wouldn't change a thing. And yes, they still have sex! Chatting to other parents is invaluable in the early days, and for men it's a reassurance that life still goes on and they haven't got to be perfect at everything to make it as a good dad. Fellowship is CRUCIAL for us all, including the guys, especially now.

Yeehah!

Stoke up your smoothie and let's take a look at the guy on the stallion. His horse is ready; he is ready. On the dusty ground lie the ropes of financial stress, the rope of worry about losing you, the rope of fear of birth. Even that rope of feeling trapped lies limp on the ground...

What's this? The horse is still not moving. Why is your man still rooted to the spot? Worries and issues that held him back may have been addressed, but somehow there is still no momentum.

Run like the wind!

There is only one thing that causes us to run, leap and chase after what is good with all our hearts. It is the wind of God's Holy Spirit. When we ask him to wash over us, fill us up entirely and breathe new life into us...then WE WILL RUN FREE!

So if the Son sets you free, you will be free indeed (John 8:36).

Time out with your Father God

The problem with Bible stories becoming well known in Sunday school is that they develop a "fairytale" ring to them and it's easy to forget that they are real accounts of actual events. Take Moses, for instance. He's the one in our toddler Bible whom my youngest mistakes for Father Christmas. Take it to the other extreme and it's easy to super-spiritualise characters such as Moses, forgetting that they were people like you and me. On the days when your own "promised land" seems out of your grasp, it can be hard to relate to such a figure. Well, let's take a snapshot of Moses' life. I suspect we might be in for a surprise.

1) Moses gets it very wrong

Moses kills a slave superintendent and gets found out by Pharaoh. He has to run. Bad move.

2) Moses' life gets very boring

For 40 long years he works as a shepherd. Our equivalent, I suppose, would be to serve burgers at McDonald's for 40 years. He must have wondered, "Is this it?" My guess is that he just got on with it (not that he had much choice). I suspect that, unbeknown to Moses, God was training him during the long wilderness years.

3) Moses can't believe God actually wants to speak to him

As Moses comes closer to the burning bush in the desert, he hears a voice say, "Moses". The voice has to say Moses' name twice because Moses can't believe God is actually speaking to him (Exodus 3:4).

4) What now?

God says to Moses, "So now, go. I am sending you..." (Exodus 3:10). I'm sure Moses must have thought "But I'm 80 years old! Surely it made more sense to send me when I was a fit, strong 40-year-old?" It's amazing, the ability we all have to question God's timing. Crazy when you look at it in the cold light of day. God knows the beginning from the end. How can we even begin to question his timing?

5) Moses tries to get out of it

"Please send someone else..." (Exodus 4:13). He feels inadequate, big time. What chance has an 80-year-old with a stick to demand the release of 2,500,000 slaves from one of the biggest world empires? It's interesting to notice here how much he must have changed during the 40 years since he swaggered around Egypt full of his own status. Those wilderness years obviously weren't wasted. Maybe God is still looking for those who know that they are weak in their own strength. They are the ones in whom he will reveal his glory.

6) What Moses doesn't know...

He doesn't know that the Red Sea will part; he doesn't know that two and a half million slaves will walk into freedom; he has no idea that he is going to deliver God's covenant to his people. He has no clue that this covenant means that Jesus (the fulfilment of the covenant) is sure to come. It is beyond Moses that God would use him to bring the concept of freedom to the world. All this is yet to come.

7) What does Moses do?

He finally responds to God's call with a "yes". He limps towards new territory with his head held high. If you say "yes" to God as he beckons you into new territory, even if you feel crippled with weakness or inadequacy, be under no illusion: God has great adventures planned for you.

> "For I know the plans I have for you," declares the Lord, "plans to prosper you and not to harm you, plans to give you hope and a future. Then you will call upon me and come to pray to me, and I will listen to you. You will seek me and find me when you seek me with all your heart. I will be found by you..." (Jeremiah 29:11–14).

Chapter 6   The Joy of Labour

OK, so now I have your attention. Calling this chapter "The Agony of Labour" might not have been quite as enticing. Maybe I should have called it "It's not over till the Fat Lady sings". I don't know about you, but for me the "fat" jokes are wearing a bit thin after nine months of girth. Anyway, I think the *joy* of labour has an "opposite extremes" ring to it that reminds me of my birth experiences...

> *"It's OK, I'm here. You can do it. Not long now. You're doing really well."* (My husband: master of the ice cubes, lord of the barley sugars.)
>
> *"Just tell them to stop this awful pain, Darren, tell them to stop this awful pain. I don't want to do this any more."* (Only I didn't say awful...)
>
> *"Shshsh. You're doing really well. Shall I rub your back?"*
> D-O-N'T T-O-U-C-H M-E
> Then minutes (hours? days?) later...
> *"Oh, Oh, Oh, Oh. Our baby! So tiny! So perfect, so beautiful..."*

That's how birth goes...joy comes from pain, relief after panic, delight after fear. It really is mind-blowing. Maybe "The Joy of Labour" is not such a far-out title after all.

Anyone found the "off" button?

Pass me any pregnancy magazine, book or even limp pam-
phlet from the doctor's and I confess that I always do the
same thing. I always flick through to the chapter on labour
and read it first. Maybe deep down I'm hoping that someone
has found the "off" button to the whole pain thing. Or maybe,
as another birth looms, I've got this crazy fascination with
anything to do with it, especially other people's birth experiences. After all, actually having a baby is what it's all about.
So if I'm not alone on this one, welcome to the chapter on
labour. Time for some high-octane action!

Joining an antenatal group

As I sat with a bunch of pregnant professionals at an antenatal
session about labour, the conversation was civilised, verging on
stilted. Chit-chat about nursery furniture, maternity leave and
Christmas shopping. At one point the robust antenatal leader
rolled up her sleeves and ploughed in with a few discussion
points: you know, the usual... pain relief, stages of labour. So
far, so good. After a bit of light discussion about labour the
conversation meandered back to Christmas and "Peter
Rabbit" layette. Minutes later, everyone was dispersing and
the bearded lady was thrusting flyers about the maternity unit
into manicured hands. Was that it? Was I the only one who
wanted to tell Peter Rabbit what he could do with his layette?
What about the real questions that bother me late at night?

Can I make labour start by mistake?
How much does it really hurt?
What if I can't do it?
What about sex?

I imagine that a bunch of pregnant women can be like any group of women who don't know each other very well. Nobody wants to make a fool of herself, so nobody is particularly honest about her hopes and fears for labour. Nobody asks the real questions that she is struggling with, and not much ground is covered. So it's down to the teacher to make sure there is plenty of opportunity, information and encouragement.

These groups can be brilliant sources of labour advice and support, and even a place where lifelong friendships are made. However, I really encourage you to do a bit of research before you join a group. What qualifications and experience does the teacher have? What topics are up for discussion? Is there a group that your friends could recommend to you? Is the leader approachable? Labour is like breastfeeding. The more preparation and support you surround yourself with, the better chance you have of a positive birth experience.

Birth experience

The whole "birth experience" concept is somewhat hard to define. For starters, everyone has different expectations of what it's going to be like. Each labour will be unique and dependent on many factors, such as your pelvis shape, how far down the baby's head is, how relaxed you are, the size of the baby, and the care you receive. There will be some women reading this book whose labour experience will rate not much higher than bad toothache. You will be the ones in your hipsters shimmying around with your pram two days after the birth. There will be lots of us who will have one heck of a painful labour followed by a normal delivery and recovery will take varying lengths of time. There will be a few of us whose labour doesn't work out as planned; we may need extra help to give birth and recovery may be longer. I was in the last category for my first two births, and I have absolutely no idea if I'll end up there again.

Actually, I think that it is the whole "unknown" nature of giving birth that makes me grasp at any snippet of information on labour that I come across. I think that deep down I'm hoping that the more information I have, the more I can get a firm idea of what could happen, and then maybe the "sense of the unknown" will go away. The only problem is that the more information I take on board, the more possibilities and outcomes there seem to be. Then the unknown seems even bigger than before.

Getting to grips with the unknown aspects of labour

I think the first step is to find out what *is* "known" about your fast-approaching birth and build on that.

1) Decide on your birth place – home or hospital. This will allow you to find out what is actually available in terms of pain relief, birth pools, etc. When you have some real options, then you are in a position to make your choices.
2) Choose your birth partner. Whether it is your husband or an experienced friend, you can discuss coping strategies and generally prepare yourselves. And don't forget cash, phone, drinks and a camera (with film!).
3) Attend all your antenatal appointments and raise your questions.

These appointments are the ideal time to fire away with all your questions. Your health and the baby's development will be carefully monitored. Should anything arise which may affect your labour, e.g. the size of the baby, you can discuss options with your caregiver.

The pregnancy taboo

Pregnant women are world experts in mentally rehearsing possible scenarios. I've got the "mummy-and-daddy-bring-baby-home" one up to Oscar-winning standard: it brings a tear to my eye every time. Unfortunately, my labour-rehearsal one kept going off at a tangent. On some days it would end with me flushed with pride as the baby gazed lovingly into my eyes. On more uncertain days I would find myself playing through a nightmare birth scenario, where everything goes wrong.

I think in our society we are often cushioned from the reality of life and death. Then, when the prospect of birth is right there in front of us, death can suddenly seem much more of a reality too. For women who have had recent experience of losing a loved one, life seems even more fragile at this time. The thought of the most precious thing in the world finally arriving can come hand in hand with the thought of not being there to see it. It's any pregnant woman's worst nightmare, and a place our progesterone-propelled imaginations may wander on a particularly vulnerable day. Let's look at this fear in the cold light of day. Yes, it does happen, but it is very, very rare. Giving birth is still safer than driving, and we do that every day. Giving birth is a normal healthy event. If your pregnancy does waver from the "norm", the obvious answer is to get good obstetric care.

I have found my life-and-death ponderings helpful in reminding me that I have only one shot at life, and that each day is precious. I am reminded that without God sustaining the universe, there would be no life. He has given us the gift of life; we really should live each day to our utmost.

Choices you can make to keep you and your baby safer

1) A balanced diet, before and during pregnancy. Before you say "Yeah, yeah, heard this one a thousand times before", wait one minute. If you think about it, every moment of every day your baby is developing bit by bit. The only fuel available for this delicate process is what you eat. It's got to be worth adding a bit of extra fruit and veg. to your plate.

   Similarly, some foods are a big no-no because they put you at risk of miscarriage. These include soft cheeses, e.g. Brie, cooked-chilled foods, and liver.

2) Keep your antenatal appointments. Monitoring your health, and your baby's health, is crucial, even if you're planning a low-key delivery. Pre-eclampsia is a top cause of maternal death, but it can be spotted and treated early if mums' blood pressure and urine are tested regularly.

3) Make sensible life choices. Save the horse-riding and saunas until after the baby is born! Wear your seatbelt when driving and start to drive as if there's a child in the car (there *is*!).

   Once you've done all you can, relax and take each day at a time. Each day is a gift in its own right.

Download the strength of heaven

No matter how much we prepare for "birth day", there is always going to be that unknown aspect stretching like a never-ending lake before us. When that reality dawns, it can feel quite daunting. Aside from arming ourselves with a good midwife to help us make good birth choices, and stocking up with a larder full of cheese sticks, there's not much else we can do but wait for D-Day. Or is there?

We have two more options to consider. We wait in fear for birth to come, or we wait in anticipation for birth to come.

Here's some fridge ministry for you (copy it out and stick it on your fridge!):

Yet if you devote your heart to him and stretch out your hands to him...you will stand firm and without fear (Job 11:13,15).

It's *Surrender Dorothy** time again. Your Father God can be trusted with your hopes, fears and dreams for birth. He knows. Allow him to ease any burden from your shoulders and rest peacefully while you wait for your special birth-day. It's your choice whether to live in trepidation of what could happen, or to download some of heaven's strength and trust in your God. Holding on to him now will train you well for your mumship.

An easy way of telling that you're operating on your own resources is that you will end up feeling utterly daunted as you contemplate labour, birth and a myriad of potential futures. When your "mum strength" is downloaded from God, you might well still feel nervous, but the icy edge of fear is no longer around your heart.

We're in miracle territory now

I'm a girl who always likes to be in the thick of things, always ready for some action. Apparently I've got something to say

---

* 1998 film by Kevin DiNovis

about everything (how did you guess?). There are two times when I can remember being utterly speechless. The first? You'll remember the moment way back in Chapter 1 when I realised that until I did the pregnancy test my baby was only known by God, as his cherished secret. That really blew me away. Another time I was utterly lost for words was when I witnessed my first birth as a student midwife. A whole new person from nothing. A wriggling bundle of life and potential. As with a lot of God's creative miracles here on earth – coral reefs, ants, birds migrating – we become accustomed to them. Let's be real here, take off the shades and pause for just a moment. God's fingerprints are all over that which he has created. Nowhere are those fingerprints more evident than in the birth of a baby.

However difficult the delivery, the miracle of birth cannot be diluted.

The moment your baby is born, the presence of your God will be almost tangible. I remember a kind of slow-motion mixture of relief, delight and awe at the miracle before my eyes. I stand in amazement that God has granted me another baby to bear. Being pregnant is truly a miracle. We may turn this way and that, run in panic or dance in the streets. We're in miracle territory now.

The question no one wants to ask

Here's a question guaranteed to put any church leader in a bit of a tizz:

If birth is a miracle from God...

A) Why does it hurt?

B) Why does it seem to go wrong fairly often?

Now this question is one I carried for a long time. Both of my previous deliveries were very traumatic and I nearly lost my baby (and indeed my own life) both times. I know Jesus is Lord of birth, so what went wrong. Was it my fault?

Let's chuck out a few myths...

You may have heard it said that miscarriage, malformation and difficult birth are caused by the sins of the mother. We all know that smoking, taking drugs and other environmental toxins DO affect the development of babies. That, however, is only half the story as far as this school of thought is concerned. I've actually read the suggestion that stillbirth is a punishment from God for the unrepented sins of the mother.

Why this myth is wrong...
God is not a cruel Father waiting to whack his children with a big stick if they step out of line. We have all sinned and come short of his standards. However, as we turn to him and say sorry, we receive forgiveness and peace rather than punishment. God is the deliverer of those under curses; he does not hand them out to his children. The Bible teaches us that sin in the world has effects on both nature and people. Droughts, famine, floods and illness are all the inevitable consequences of a world turning its back on its Creator. The Bible also teaches that we are all sinners, fallen short of God's standard of acceptance. Jesus' death on the cross was an acceptable sacrifice before God, so that those who repent of their sins and turn to him are made utterly welcome in God's family. Becoming his child does not, however, mean that we are immune to sickness, pain and loss while we're still on the earth. We are still living in that same world that has turned its back on him. When we reach heaven, all sickness and pain will disappear.

Pain-free birth?

Physical pain in general is due to sin entering the world. This includes childbirth, according to the book of Genesis (Genesis 3:16). We now know that Jesus has conquered sin, so the power of sin no longer has dominion over us. Therefore, is it not possible for a Christian to give birth without the pain? Tempted as I am, on approaching my third delivery, to launch into a barrage of "free-me-from-pain" prayers, there's just one thought that is stopping me. Rather than chasing a pain-free birth, should I not be using my energy to chase God himself?

There is pain at times of great passion; God didn't make a race of robots. Did Mary not cry out in pain as she gave birth to Jesus? I think she did. The pain of birth is different from the pain of death. It is a positive, live-giving process. Maybe God shouted in the heavens as he created and birthed the world. The contractions of labour are all-consuming and it is impossible to focus on anything else. The experience of labour shuts out the rest of the world. I remember it felt as if I was back at that secret place with just God, me and the baby. Labour focuses you on an event of huge significance. The pain is life-giving and goes both physically and emotionally deep. In the Old Testament, God's people gave cries of victory and blew on their horns as they advanced into the new land that God had given them. Embarking on parenthood is entering promised-land territory, as we discussed in the chapter on fatherhood. I think labour is a fitting time to cry out in victory and for help from the Lord.

How do I cope with the contractions?

Mental strategies

Have you noticed that birth-speak is peppered with what sound like made-up words? You know, like meconium (sounds like instant coffee), Kitzinger (bless her!), epidural (got to be motor oil). Well, I thought I'd throw a word of my own into the melting pot of birth-speak – "tsunami". OK, so you may think that the pregnant woman on the laptop has had one too many sardine smoothies and has finally lost the plot. Bear with me.

The tsunami strategy of labour survival

Contractions come in waves that peak and trough. They start as little waves, lapping the shore, and gradually build up in intensity. Before you know it the waves are almost over-whelming, the sea is rough, and it seems that you'll never ever reach the shore on the other side. They just keep on com-ing, relentlessly. Help!

This is where the "tsunami" strategy fits in. Tsunami is the Japanese word for "giant wave". A tsunami makes even tidal waves look tiny in comparison. It is the big momma of all waves. A tsunami begins far out in the ocean, its momen-tum gathering. Unlike a tidal wave, it cannot be seen until it reaches the shore. This is because it gains its speed, power and force as it silently moves along the ocean bed. All that can be seen on the surface are a few large waves that feed its momentum; nothing to hint at the ultimate power about to swallow all the waves and crash to the shore.

Back to the strategy. As each contraction wave hit, I imag-ined it was merely building the deep wave of momentum in my heart: a tsunami of determination, love and God's strength that would carry me to the shore when I could do no more. This mental focus really made a difference to my ability to handle the contractions. I imagined that I could "cash in" my tsunami at any time to overwhelm the contraction waves. This knowledge gave me a sense of control and made me more determined to hold on, hold on and save the momentum for when the baby was to be born. When that point finally came, even though for me it ended up in the theatre with an emergency C-section, I remained focused and cashed in my tsunami with a surge of determination and victory as the baby was born. It worked for me.

I strongly recommend that you get yourself a coping strategy; use tsunami or make up one of your own. My friend imagined that each contraction was a step coming up out of a cellar. The steps led to a door which opened onto a beautiful garden as the baby was born.

Physical strategy
We all have different needs in labour, and it is hard to predict which strategies will help and which will not. Some women find that a physical touch from someone else is really soothing and comforting. I'm afraid I'm more of the "D-O-N'T T-O-U-C-H M-E" type. This left my poor bewildered husband clutching the flannel and ice until he found a new role in providing his hand for me to crush.

The position you adopt through the whole birth process can make a huge difference to the pain and even ease of delivery. Upright positions such as standing, kneeling and squatting mean that gravity is on your side, which has to be a bonus. Being able to move freely during birth, many women say, is a strong instinct and gives a better sense of control and focus. When it comes to the actual delivery, standing, kneeling or squatting in particular open the pelvis up much more widely than other positions, thus lowering your risk of needing intervention to get the baby out.

How will my body know what to do?

The physical process of birth is outrageously amazing in the sheer order and accuracy of its progress. How does the womb know what to do? How do the contractions know to start when the waters break? How do the womb muscles know how to contract regularly? How does the placenta know when it is time to detach from the womb and be delivered? It is an intricate process, a whole-body effort. Our bodies are utterly amazing machines.

As women, we so often focus on how our bodies look from the outside – how we look, what shape we are. We even try to eat healthily just to get the outside to look better. If we merely focus on how good or bad we look, our self-image can become rather shallow. The intricate process of giving birth has left me open-mouthed (again). My body is amazing: so much more than how big my bum looked, or whether I could get away with eating a chocolate biscuit. It's all too easy never to look below the surface and give the body the respect it deserves. I didn't really, until the process of birth sort of woke me up. If we really took hold of the miracle that is our bodies growing a baby, I'm sure we would have a self-respect far deeper than that of our non-childbearing sisters.

Time out with your Father God

Giving birth is "hello" and "goodbye" all wrapped up in one big package. It's goodbye to life as you knew it, and hello to a new little person and a whole new adventure. You don't get a much more significant life event than that!

The equivalent in the jungle track of your Christian journey is taking the step of getting baptised. This is a brilliant step, when you tell the whole world that you say "goodbye" to your old life, when Jesus meant nothing to you, and "hello" to a new start, when he means everything to you. A chance to be "born again"! Just like giving birth, taking the step of baptism can be daunting, and you could easily let fear get in the way. And just like giving birth, baptism was God's idea and a significant life event full of blessing for you.

If you've not been baptised and you love Jesus, I urge you to take the step while you are still pregnant. What better time could there be for a fresh start? What better way of abandoning all your crutches and calling out to God? What better witness to your friends and family? What better way to stand as a new family before earth and heaven and blow your victory horn?

Peter replied, "Repent and be baptised, every one of you, in the name of Jesus Christ for the forgiveness of your sins" (Acts 2:38).

Chapter 7   How to Have a Delicious, Inspiring Home (God in the House!)

There's something surreal and dreamlike about actually driving home with your baby for the very first time. I remember sitting in the back seat trying desperately to resist the temptation to tell my husband to slow down/watch the traffic lights/mind the manholes. We made it halfway home with no drama. You know what's coming next. Baby starts to wail inconsolably. Parents exchange frozen looks through the rear-view mirror. Parents experience a knot in stomach. Driver speeds up slightly. Traditionally, at a time like this, all new parents feel their stomachs churn and experience shallow breathing. We didn't break with tradition. Minutes later (felt like hours) we made it to our house. AT LAST. As soon as we took the car seat out and walked towards the door, Joseph stopped crying as if by magic. RELIEF. We gave each other knowing looks that said "He knows he's home, that's why he's stopped crying". OK, maybe it was more to do with the icy wind momentarily taking his breath away, but remember that new parents are sleep-deprived and welcome any shred of logic, sentimental or not. We stumbled through that familiar doorway convinced that our baby was pleased to be home. It felt really good. We'd got high hopes for home life.

High hopes

Now I've got a couple of little ones, my expectations of home life are still high. I want so much for our home to be a place full of calm, not chaos, laughter, not shouting. I want home to be a place of fun memories and happy times. I'm sure you share those hopes and dreams for your family. Actually achieving our goals for home life can sometimes feel like an uphill battle, like that slippery bar of soap. Stuff gets in the way. Then resentment sets in, and we find ourselves in a rut we never wanted to be in. Whatever you come home to, being pregnant makes it more of an issue. Why? Because deep down you know this is it. A little person is going to get in on the act here very soon. Also, you need to feel safe and secure during this roller coaster that is pregnancy. Home matters.

Stuff

Sometimes STUFF gets in the way of my home being the place of relaxation and peace that I want it to be. "Stuff" is anything that robs us of our peace and leaves us in chaos, e.g.

- Clutter, no space anywhere
- Boredom with chores and the general monotony of housework
- Frustration at other family members
- Rushing all the time

What a depressing list! Well, if you've ever felt frustration at any of the above, it's stuff-busting time. Pregnant or not, it's time to get up, start to deal with the stuff that robs us of peace in our homes, and nail those gremlins. If you don't, no one else will. Let's live a little and enjoy home life. A peaceful home really is within our grasp.

Should you feel that there could be even the teensiest bit of room for improvement in the running of your home, then read on. What have you got to lose?

Peace-stealer number one: clutter

We all get stuck in a rut if our homes slip into bad shape. When all you see is clutter, you can't settle in the space. Clutter causes us to have an uneasy feeling and we feel unable to relax completely. What is clutter? Look in any self-help manual and the answer is there in black and white: anything that doesn't make you smile, or have a regular function in your house, counts as clutter.

Why do I have such an almighty bee in my bonnet about this whole clutter issue? Believe it or not, it is an issue that God has put his finger on in my life. No, I'm no particularly a hoarder; I have my organised days and my not so organised days (more of these). However, I had a sense of unease that seemed to linger whenever I was at home. Frustration at not being able to find things, and occasionally being mortified if someone arrived at the house unexpectedly. I prayed. This is what I learned about clutter in my life:

1) Clutter was there because I hadn't moved on from the past (keeping ALL my old Uni notes, books I had once enjoyed but would never read again, paperwork that I didn't actually need).

2) Clutter was there because I wasn't dealing with things. I had letters to reply to, broken things that needed fixing, things that hadn't been put away.

3) Clutter was there because I did more dreaming than action (lots of home improvement manuals, home business magazines, clothes I would only fit into if I was two stones lighter).

With clutter, I was stuck in the past or dreaming about the future without ever having to deal with the here and now. God wants me to live in his provision for the here and now. God wants me as I am. Not bound by "what I could have been", not even striving for what I might be. Raw me, right now, trusting in him. He'll deal with the rest. That revelation was liberating beyond belief.

Peace-stealer number two: lifestyle-chasing

Clutter multiplies when we chase lifestyles and become dissatisfied. A big part of being happy in life is being thankful for what you do have. If we find ourselves regularly thinking about having a bigger house, a better car, or nicer furniture, we are never going to be fulfilled. So we buy stuff to make ourselves feel better. Clutter increases. Let's give this way of living the boot. Let's be happy with what we do have.

My gran was a tea-cosy, nylon-knickers kind of gran. She reused envelopes and even cut legs off old tights to make stockings in the warm weather. Never would I have dreamed that she would have put her finger on the secret of a happy home life. No, it's not about being careful and thrifty, not even about making good use of what you have. It's certainly not about nylon gussets. Here's the secret:

Do not store up for yourselves treasures on earth, where moth and rust destroy... But store up for yourselves treasure in heaven (Matthew 6:19,20).

It's about where you put your heart, your energies and your focus. As we discussed in the chapter about priorities, it's about learning to be a peace-chaser, rather than being a lifestyle-chaser.

Peace-stealer number three: it's not fair!

It sounds very petty, but it's so easy to slip into this mentality, especially when you've got a baby. It's easy to lose the plot. Marriage is not a 50/50 deal. It's a 100/100 gift.

The "it's not fair" mentality is a real marriage-crippler. The way to break the cycle? Stop keeping a score. Give love, over and over again. I'm getting to grips with this hard lesson as I'm finally realising how unconditionally God loves me. He never keeps the score on my mistakes; he keeps on loving me even when I am hard-hearted. I am learning to soften my heart, to let go of the pride and love as I am loved by God. I am learning to treasure my husband.

Peace-stealer number four: leaking paint

Remember those days of running around like a headless chicken, exhausted yet not achieving anything? This will bring a smile to your face... I saw a line-marking lorry on the road the other day that was leaking paint. So, for every perfectly straight line painted on the road, it also left behind a parallel wavy line. The driver was so intent on his straight lines that he didn't look behind his lorry to see what was going on and sort out his leak. Sometimes we concentrate so hard on the things requiring our immediate attention that we don't take a moment to step back, take a longer look, and check for any leaks. I find that stepping out of the normal routine of life for a few hours is the best way to mull over things. A walk in the woods, a sauna, a wander by a lake, even an evening in the bath are all prime activities that allow you to switch off, reboot and look at where your time and effort are going. It's amazing what a stress-reliever simply getting away from things for a short while actually is.

Peace-stealer number five: bored, bored, bored!

Washing clothes, doing dishes, tidying toys, making beds, cleaning the floor, hanging the washing out, mowing the lawn. Boring, Boring, Boring. Or *is* it? Prepare for some radical thinking...

When we look upon these chores as work, we hate doing them. Change your attitude from drudgery to pleasure. When you do things for your family, and to your home, you are giving them a tangible chunk of your love. A clean shirt is like a kiss for your husband; a hot meal after school is like a hug for your seven-year-old. A tidy living room for when you come down in the morning is like leaving yourself a box of chocolates. Let go of any resentment and nurture your family with kindness. Again, we're not talking rocket science here. I'm not the first to start thinking like this. It doesn't have to be mundane. Put on some funky music, wear a smile, pray as you clean, have a painting party – it's up to you. Above all, love your home so it is fit to receive your baby. Allow it to be a place where you reach your destiny in God, a place that becomes a springboard for your child. A place where your whole family will flourish. A delicious, inspiring, safe place. God is in the house!

Seven steps to a delicious, inspiring, happy home

With a little "stuff-busting" under your belt, can I tempt you to read on a bit further and have a go at a few of these seven steps I've got lined up? I take absolutely no credit for these steps; they are straight from the book of Proverbs. Allow me to introduce the wife of noble character:

> A wife of noble character who can find? She is worth far more than rubies (Proverbs 31:10–31).

Wow! Why is she so valued? What is her secret? She has seven secrets, actually. They are:

1) She treasures her husband

> She brings him good, not harm, all the days of her life (v 12).

She chooses not to nag, or manipulate. She makes a positive choice to treasure him EVERY day (not just the days when things are going well). She is kind-hearted and committed to him. She initiates (she brings him good); she does not wait for him to bring her things first.

2) She makes careful choices

> She selects wool and flax and works with eager hands (v 13).

> She considers a field and buys it; out of her earnings she plants a vineyard (v 16).

She chooses carefully where to put her energies, then gives it her very best. In these verses we see the confidence with which the wife works to meet her chosen goal. Full throttle. It takes guts not to carry a rucksack of doubts with you wherever you go. She plans ahead, not just living for the moment. It takes bravery to venture into the unknown territory of motherhood; we won't make a success of it if we just plough on without thinking about where we put our energies.

3) She is not fearful

> When it snows, she has no fear for her household; for all of them are clothed in scarlet (v 21).

I imagine her family all snuggled together under a scarlet velvet cloak as the icy wind chills their cheeks and the snow falls around them. Yet they're not afraid. They're warm and safe under the cloak. I imagine the scarlet cloak as representing the blood of Jesus, with healing, comforting, restoring power. We sew this cloak for our households with every prayer, every caring touch and every wise decision. The blood of Jesus casts out all fear.

I had to put this scripture into action one afternoon last year. I was cooking tea for my toddler, Joseph, when I had to leave the kitchen to rescue baby Samuel who had got his car stuck in the fire guard. Minutes later, vehicle rescue was successfully achieved and I returned to the kitchen. There I found the cooker engulfed in flames. I rang for emergency help and dashed barefooted into the street clutching my babies. I stood helplessly, watching the smoke get thicker. Then, somehow, I remembered the verse:

When it snows, she has no fear for her household; for all of them are clothed in scarlet (v 21).

I felt strength well up in me. Our little home was too precious to be destroyed by fire, and I wasn't going to just stand by and watch. So, with all the strength I could muster, I shouted, "In the name of Jesus, fire, be gone." And the fire suddenly diminished. Seriously high flames just disappeared. A minute later there was a frantic rush of activity as two fire engines rolled up and neighbours started coming out of their houses. The smoke damage was everywhere, but only I knew how much worse it could have been. God had heard my cry. My prayer had covered our home in scarlet.

4) She manages her home

She watches over the affairs of her household... (v 27).

A calm home doesn't just happen. It takes hard work, underpinned with making time for each other. Planning the affairs of a house alleviates stress, as does making time for fun, outings and family meals. Compare these two scenarios:

It's 5.30pm; you've no idea what's for tea. The kids are hungry, so you go and get a takeaway. Later you feel guilty as you consider your expanding waistline and expanding overdraft.

It's 5.30pm. You took 20 minutes the other day to plan the meals for the coming week. Tonight is Tuesday and it's chilli and salad. You've already got what you need and it's simmering away, so you sit down for a well-earned cup of tea and read a magazine until it is ready.

Which scenario is less stressful?

Just for the record, I love takeaways. But aren't they so

much more pleasurable when they are a treat (planned *or* spontaneous) rather than a panic purchase? There is a world of difference between spontaneity and having no direction.

5) She chooses her words carefully

> She speaks with wisdom, and faithful instruction is on her tongue (v 26).

Children are like soft clay. How they feel about themselves, and how they approach the world, is shaped by how we talk to them. Words are one of the most powerful parenting tools that we have.

Do we really realise the impact that our words have? It's all too easy to meander along, saying what we think, and fire-fighting along the way. I think I do it sometimes. However, I have a sneaking suspicion that a golden, diamond-encrusted key to a happy home life lies in the realm of our words. Just imagine if this was our motto, stuck to the fridge:

> May the words of my mouth and the meditation of my heart be pleasing in your sight, O Lord, my Rock and my Redeemer (Psalm 19:14).

Just imagine if we softened our hearts and kept a tight rein on what comes out of our mouths. Dare we even imagine the impact on our households if we did such a thing with God's help? Would rivers of mercy, life and hope come cascading down the stairs and touch every heart in every room, every day? Imagine it if we no longer rose to arguments and no longer criticised...

Oh, sweet Jesus, touch our hearts. Let our words be like rivers of honey through our homes. Soften our hearts.

6) She's no navel-gazer

> She opens her arms to the poor and extends her hands to the needy (v 20).

We all get caught up in our own little world to some degree when we have a baby on the way. It's those pregnancy-tinted glasses again. Even the most mundane things can become a worry should they affect any of our pregnancy plans. I think that our friend the noble wife would have been no different when she was pregnant. However, she doesn't keep her passion just for her own little family. She cares passionately for others. I suspect she even had a soft heart towards those who were hard-hearted towards her.

7) Let it rip!

> She makes coverings for her bed... (v 22).

> She makes linen garments and sells them... (v 24).

The noble wife indulged her creativity and ingenuity. I took up writing when I was newly pregnant with my first baby. There was something about having a new life within me that made me want to try new things. Somehow, being pregnant gave me a sense that anything was possible. Creativity is a choice you make. Go on, indulge yourself!

Time out with your Father God

> Charm is deceptive, and beauty is fleeting; but a woman who fears the Lord is to be praised (Proverbs 31:30).

A woman who fears the Lord will know his touch on her children, her husband and her family life. "Fearing the Lord" simply means giving God the respect and glory due to him, whatever's going on in our lives. It's for the days that are full of sunshine and for the days when it seems as if our world is collapsing around us. He is still worthy of our love and adoration. Yes, even on those days.

Chapter 8   Making Good Choices is Easier than You Think

Pregnant women have one thing in common with trainspotters, computer freaks and motorbike enthusiasts. They all relish even the tiniest snippet of information on their current passion. Even standing in the queue at the minimarket can be mildly interesting for a pregnant woman. Sneaking a peak at other people's maternity clothes/method of disciplining their two-year-old/style of car-seat cover can take the boredom out of standing in any queue. Then of course there's the age-old game of working out how flat a mother's stomach is in relation to the age of the baby (this last one will reach a whole new level of interest after you've had your baby). Indeed, what in the world could be more fascinating to think about than having a baby? You find yourself wondering what your baby's face will look like, what you'll say at the birth, whether your baby will like your mother-in-law. Even in a traffic jam it's all too easy to find yourself working out the genetic probability of ginger hair, or which brand of breast pump would best fit in your drawer at work.

Pregnancy brain overhaul

A further progression of this pregnancy brain overhaul is the "I've got to have it now, and I mean *now*" mentality when it comes to food and drink. I challenge anyone to get in front of a pregnant woman as she opens the fridge. Maybe there's a biological explanation for it all; your man will know exactly what I'm talking about if he's ever dared eat your last peach melba yoghurt/tin of chickpeas/packet of chocolate biscuits. This complete brain overhaul has got to be nature's way of making the baby priority number one.

There are two good things about this pregnancy obsession. Firstly, a year or so down the line it will give you some cracking stories to laugh over with any girlfriends who have also had babies. I've had many a side-splitting evening with a couple of friends, reminiscing about our pregnancy quirks. Definitely more entertaining than swapping birth stories.

Secondly, it's rather nice to have a little universe belonging only to you and your baby. I relished the realisation that I was changing, and starting to think a bit like a mum and not just me. I felt a sense of God's destiny, plans and hopes for me. I was still really daunted, but absolutely smitten.

> *In the sheltered simplicity of the first days after a baby is born, one sees again the magical closed circle, the miraculous sense of two people existing only for each other...*
> (Anne Morrow Lindbergh, b. 1901)

How many other relationships are as memorable or significant? You are your baby's universe. Bearing children is more mind-blowing than walking on Mars, travelling the world or surpassing your ambitions. So then, why has the popularity of mothering taken such a spectacular nosedive in the last 30 years?

Priorities versus demands

Whatever your granny might say about mobiles, dishwashers and Internet shopping, it's a tough call being a wife and mother in today's society. There are so many demands on your every waking minute. It's so easy to find yourself shunted along by the circumstances and pressures of modern life. Making decisions about priorities in life is never easy, but when there is a never-ending list of things vying for your attention, it's tricky to know which way to turn next. To top it all, these pressures increase during the nine months of your life when your hormones are working overtime and your outgoings are sky-rocketing from baby purchases. It might not get as bad as feeling you have to choose between your life and the baby, but for some women it feels as if compromises have to be made, if only to ease the sense of pressure. Should you quit work/your role as gymnastics coach/your regular nights out with the girls? Or is it right for you and the baby to suddenly be chained to the kitchen sink for the next 18 years? Choices, choices, choices. Enough to send the most maternal of us on a retail-therapy frenzy. So, before you hotfoot it to Monsoon clutching your credit card, let's take a well-deserved break for just a minute. Grab yourself a parsnip sandwich or a chickpea sundae and come on a virtual adventure with me...

Just imagine...

Imagine one of those sailing ships of old, complete with rigging, sails, creaking timbers and anchor. There's an ocean blue, an undiscovered island in the distance, rushing wind...you get the idea. The island on the horizon is certainly looking good. Sandy beach, palm trees, treasure chests of jewels, a table laden with every tropical fruit you can imagine.

Feeling chilled yet? Now, let's take a virtual trip together to that beautiful sailing ship. You're standing in the crow's nest, high up between the top two sails. The wind is rushing through your hair, just like in the film *Titanic*. You can smell the sea and feel the sun beating down on your shoulders. You feel confident because this is your ship, and you're directing the skipper below as to which sail to raise, which way to turn the wheel to steer your vessel swiftly to that undiscovered island in the distance.

Now here's the good bit. The ship represents your life; she's expertly carved, has weathered both rocky and calm seas, and has been declared seaworthy by the master builder. The island of treasures on the horizon represents the destiny God has for your life – the good things he has for you. Gifts and provision from an extravagant, abundant God who has fresh fruit, warm sand and restful hammocks for you. Oh yes, there is also true contentment to be found hovering over the clear waters by the shore. So how do you guide your ship there?

Let's pretend that each sail on the ship represents a chunk of your life... relationship with God, your husband, relationship with family, work commitments, church commitments, friendships, hobbies, etc. Everyone's ship has a different combination of sails. Why not grab a pen and scribble on a bit of paper what you would have written on each of these sails? These are the things vying for your time and energy throughout the day. These are the things that you have to prioritise. As you raise these sails in the right order, prioritising where you put your time, energy and focus, the wind of God will blow the ship of your life to the island of treasures. You will be happy, and even a turbulent sea will not force you off course. So to the crux of it. How do you know which sails to raise? How do you decide what takes priority in your life? Raising the sails in no particular order would result in the ship merely spinning around in the water and not actually making any progress at all. So, is prioritising your sails in life the ultimate slippery bar of soap on a rope? The "krypton factor" that is impossible to solve? How do you know what God would have you do?

Here's an idea... Ask yourself, "Is this sail, this part of my life, something that God gave me, or did I initiate it without him?" "Is it something the Bible regards as good?" In other words – has it got God's fingerprints all over it, or not? I'm not necessarily talking about church things, either. Thinking these questions through helped me to identify the things I was involved in that I needed to let go of. They were eating away at me, rather than building me up. It's really important to find out which are the sails that need to be taken off the rigging, as they will only hinder the journey to the island. Cross them off the list, see what it feels like.

> A time to search and a time to give up, a time to keep and a time to throw away (Ecclesiastes.3:6).

Now you have remaining the sails, or areas of your life, that have positive potential for you. The sea in which you sail may be choppy or calm at the moment. Putting up the right sails will get you to that island whatever your sea is like. Your sails will probably now include your family, your home and probably your job/other roles outside the home. So, how do you prioritise these sails so that raising one doesn't cancel out another? How do you find the best way to allot your time, energy and focus? OK, let's look at the God-priority first (don't skip this bit!).

Top priority

Let's cut to the chase on this one...

> Question: WHY is obeying God top priority?
>
> Answer: Because he is worthy of our every breath. He is the Lord. If we try to do things our own way, pulling against what the Bible teaches as right, we will be dishonouring him. We will be denying him his rightful place in our lives, and we will not be happy.

Give me understanding, and I will keep your law and obey it with all my heart. Direct me in the path of your commands, for there I find delight. Turn my heart towards your statutes and not towards selfish gain. Turn my eyes away from worthless things; preserve my life according to your word (Psalm 119:34–37).

We will end up confused and frustrated if we don't come to him. If we don't read the Bible, our hearts become a junk receptacle filled with whatever happens to be around. Not a good move.

The earwig factor

Six weeks before my first baby was due, I noticed an earwig meandering across my kitchen sink. I know I should have been kind and put it outside, but I confess I washed it down the sink without a second thought. I went back to the sofa and put the TV on; even snooker can be mildly interesting when you're in pregnant-whale mode. There, across the screen, were another couple of earwigs, and – you guessed it – there was one on the remote when I reached for it. I squashed all three thoroughly, but that crunching sound did nothing to allay my sense of unease. Remember, I turn into a real hygiene freak when pregnant, and insects in my home were definitely not on the agenda. The next morning, after crunching another dozen earwigs in the kitchen, and four IN MY BED, I snapped. I had had enough. I collected every squashed earwig that I had killed that morning and lined them up on the kitchen windowsill till it looked like a war zone. "There," I said triumphantly. "That'll make any other earwigs think twice about coming into my home!" Unfortunately, the next batch of earwigs to come sauntering along didn't learn from their relatives' fate, and they didn't stay away. Rentokil had to do the deed.

Now the chances of earwigs learning from their mistakes are pretty remote. Let's not be earwigs when it comes to decision-making! Let's not be blind to the possible consequences of our choices, good or bad. Don't stack up choices now that you will regret in the future. Holding on to God at the decision-making stage will guard you from making regrettable mistakes. Life is not a dress rehearsal.

Before I was pregnant, I found it quite fun observing others make parenting choices – noting their mistakes, smugly thinking how I would do things differently. Now it's my turn to have turbo-charged offspring and I've quickly realised how tricky this parenting business can be. It's not as easy as it looks.

A real hot potato

The issue of working when you have a young family is a real hot potato today, and is often not discussed. Well, don't worry, we can handle it. Stoke up your sardine smoothie and let's take a high-octane tour of the "work and baby" issue right now.

Juggling is what motherhood is all about, isn't it? Indeed, I am currently typing this with one hand and with the other I am demonstrating the art of playdough sausage-making to my persistent toddler. Every women's magazine seems to have the word "juggle" on every page. Oh yes, juggling is part of the picture in motherhood, and I expect it has been throughout history. You ask the mother with her baby in a sling in a paddy field; you ask the home-schooling mum of five who lives near me. There are many families for whom the mother working is the only way to feed hungry mouths and keep the roof over their heads, survival. Single mums have to provide for all their family's needs, with no one to share the burden. What a job. I think there's something awesome that happens when a child grows up knowing that Mummy trusts in God for all their needs.

Regardless of your domestic situation, you may feel real pressure to have a job when you have a young family simply to prove that you're still a person to be reckoned with. You are very much expected to invest yourself in your career, and enjoy the rewards. I've seen so many women shunted along by these pressures without even realising it. It takes a lot of courage to step back for a moment and assess things. What are you investing yourself in? Does it have God's fingerprints all over it? Are you trying to keep others happy at the expense of the right choice for you?

These questions are just as relevant for stay-at-home mums... over-busying yourself with "stuff", whether it be housework, DIY, teaching French, seeing friends, whatever. Again, there are pressures to prove yourself and have something to show for your time "off". The point is that both work and other interests can draw your passion and focus away from your baby if you don't keep tabs on things.

Here's a thought on the issue of working when you have little ones:

The crucial point is not whether there is an outside job/interest in the schedule, but what's most important in the schedule. Where does the focus of the day lie?

Put your heart and passion into the priority sail God has given you: your new family. You unfurl this sail to its full breadth, even if it seems weak and stiff, and your God will be faithful to you and blow his Spirit into the sail. Now is your season to love your family with all your passion and energy. Many women have successfully slotted in work around their main priorities.

So far, I've found staying at home more rewarding than I could have possibly imagined. Of course there are days when I don't enjoy it one bit; sometimes it's lonely and utterly exhausting. But I have had the privilege of seeing my little ones' first steps, and heard their first word. We have had picnics in the snow, read the story of Robin Hood in the depths of Sherwood forest, buried boxes of treasure on the beach, and even kept ants and watched them tunnel.

I have friends who work outside the home, and they remain fully devoted to their family. I know a mum who gets up at 5.45am every weekday so that she can have a whole hour just cuddling and reading to her daughter before the busy time when everyone is getting ready to go out. Combining mothering a little one and full-time work is possible, but it is perhaps one of the most stressful life choices there is. If you absolutely have to work, do it as well as mothering, not *instead of* mothering. You are a precious resource. You are mummy.

"Poor old me..."

Many of us have looked at the sails in our lives, e.g. family, home, life situations, and have thought that if only they were different then it would be easier to love them. Some of us feel that we drew the short straw on some things, so why should we be giving them high priority? It's time to throw this "poor-old-me" attitude away. For years I didn't clean a particular cupboard in my kitchen because it was so broken and hard to reach that it reminded me of how tiny and difficult my kitchen was compared to my friends' kitchens. I felt hard done by, so the proud bit in me refused to get on my knees, reach in and clean the thing. OK, that's just a kitchen cupboard, but that attitude is far more destructive if you look at your husband and secretly wish he was different. "If he pulled his finger out and actually came out with me without moaning about it then I'd be more inclined to iron his shirts...". "If he listened to me more then maybe I'd take the time to pray for him...". "What's the point in me taking his car through the car wash when he just leaves sweet wrappers in it all the time?"

What love is really about

God didn't call us to pour our everything into marriage only when things are perfect. There's a mum I spoke to last year who struggled alone in church every Sunday with four children all crawling all over her, because her husband just wouldn't come to church. She sat every Sunday with tears stinging her eyes, feeling lonely and empty. Then she told me that she chose to soften her heart, and allow God to change her. She started to sing her heart out to the Lord, to give thanks. She girded herself up to be the watchwoman on the wall of her family. She asked God for a tender heart; she cried out to him for her family. She gave herself to her husband wholeheartedly. She said that she tried to stop criticising and commenting on what he does; instead, she lifted him up. That's what love is about.

The mums who have the least fun

There are lots of bad rumours about parenting: you have no time for yourself; the kids will have more of a social life than you; you won't get a minute's peace... None of these have to be true: parenting can be the best fun you'll ever have. Sometimes the mums who have the least fun are those who are so giving and self-sacrificing to their children that their own self-esteem and relationships with others suffer for it.

> *I don't understand where I'm going wrong. I've just finished redecorating Sophie's room and making a three-tier cake for Max's first birthday. I've given up my pottery class so I can help out at Sophie's playgroup in the afternoons. I know I need to lose weight but we're trying for a baby (we want close gaps) so I guess I'll have to put that off till after pregnancy. I don't see as much of Keith these days, he works a fair bit. We only seem to talk about the kids then go to bed.*

The above example, unlike the others in this book, is not a real person. Can you see where our virtual friend is going wrong? She hasn't got round to unfurling her own sail to the fresh breeze. You will not be doing yourself, or your baby, any favours by meeting his or her every need but denying yourself any pleasure or time out. Self-respect is a crucial part of God's plan for mothers of our generation. A definite priority sail in our boat. Looking after yourself makes you happier and more giving, as you are not drained all the time. Looking after your marriage reminds you that you are a valued and attractive adult. You have a sense of stability that enables you to relax and you have enough growth and development to enable you still to feel like an interesting person.

No more headless chicken

I suspect that the key to the priority of self-respect for a new mum is having boundaries. Allotting time for things you want to be done, time for friendships, and time for indulging yourself. Having routines is a way of making sure that the important things get done without running around like a headless chicken. There are definitely two types of people in this world when it comes to being organised.

There are those who are born organised and naturally have routines and systems so that their life is as hassle-free as possible. They prefer jobs to be done properly and tend to have fairly tidy homes. These women have an advantage on the new-baby front in that they naturally prioritise and don't allow everything to build up too much. They may feel at a disadvantage though when it comes to wholeheartedly following the baby's needs, as there is no sense of routine during the early weeks. The baby will wake and need attention at any time in the day or night, and born-organised mothers may find "going with the flow" a bit disorientating.

Those of us who are more "organisationally challenged" and prefer to go with the flow may well breeze through the chaos of the early weeks, but feel out of our depth when the washing builds up, the car keys seem to have disappeared, and there's no loo roll left. My friend Liz was so disorientated after feeding little Caleb that when someone called round with a present in their work attire, she said, "Working late, then?"

but it was actually 9 o'clock in the morning. Eating cornflakes for dinner three nights running can do this to anyone.

Frenzy versus calm

In my BC (Before Children) days I was quite proud of my go-with-the-flow approach to life. I could juggle at an amazing rate and I thought I was pretty good under pressure. What I didn't realise, however, was that the chaos, juggling and stress that I thought I was so good at negotiating through was my own doing in the first place. I'd miss breakfast because I had to iron something to wear, then stop to get a roll to eat on the way to work, get caught in a queue at the shop, then end up almost late. I'd crisis-clean the house in a "mother-in-law's-coming" type of frenzy, humping the vacuum cleaner around the house, dusting the tops of wardrobes, scrubbing the floor to within an inch of its life, only to do nothing for days and watch it all build up again worse than before. I suppose that, in my passion for enjoying life, I thought that life was too short for me to limit it by having routines.

What I didn't realise was that by prioritising my day, whacking in a few routines here and there and even getting my clothes ready the night before (shock!), life suddenly felt so much less fraught, chaotic and stressful. A small vetting of priorities each day keeps things on an even keel, and this is something you'd give a serious amount of cash for when your baby comes home.

There is no getting away from the fact that God is a God of order. The seasons, the cycles of nature, and, of course, pregnancy show that things have a time and a place and a structure. Interestingly, there is no striving or difficulty for nature's order to occur. Just look at the tides, the movement of the planets, the growth of a tiny flower... each step happens in order. Even snowflakes have pattern and structure. Beauty in nature is closely interwoven with order. I suspect that if we submit ourselves to God's priorities, and have his order to our lives, the beauty only glimpsed in a snowflake or a rainbow will be ours in full measure. I've included being organised as a priority "sail" for you to unfurl on your life-ship in this chapter because nurturing yourself is crucial if you want to nurture your family.

Time out with your Father God

Maybe the answer to getting priorities sorted out is simply to wait on God, read the Bible and bask in his company. Do some God-bathing. If decisions are still to hard to make, choose a wise Christian friend and ask for advice. The early years build the foundation of family life; it's got to be worth making the right choices.

> In all your ways acknowledge him, and he will make your paths straight (Proverbs 3:6).

Chapter 9   Life with a New Baby (The Real Story!)

At last we had our baby. We were exhausted, dazzled, thirsty, and a dazed version of happy. My husband sort of hugged my elbow (the only bit of me that he could get to) and I sort of hugged the baby. I dozed off, dreaming of the weeks to come... taking him home... showing him off to the grandparents...trips to the park... sleepy snuggles... rocket boobs... cracked nipples... no sleep... 3am scream-offs... paracetamol syrup in the remote. Oh! Thank goodness it was only a dream. Well, back to reality. Where were we?

Oh yes, the delivery room. There I was, drifting off into well-earned sleep, baby slumbering in his perspex cocoon. All was well with the world. I stirred as the midwife gently suggested that I feed the baby. I had waited a long time for this moment; I was up for it. Gingerly I shuffled towards the cot, trying to ignore the suspicion that my post-birth tummy was actually buffing the floor. I picked up my bundle; he gazed at me as if I were the most wonderful creature in the world. My husband turned and looked at me as if I were the most wonderful creature in the world. I could get used to this. I started to feed him. Maybe I was cut out for this after all; I *felt* like the most wonderful creature in the world. Four hours later I was still sitting there, only by then I was just feeling like a cow with stretch marks.

Three days later I was home, and he was still going for

the longest first feed in history. A week later he was still feeding, and I was past noticing whether my coffee was hot or
cold. Each day blurred into the next. I dashed to the shops for
essentials between feeds and it was days before I noticed that
I had put the loo roll in the fridge and the milk in the bathroom cupboard. I could never remember which breast's turn
it was to feed, so I resorted to drawing a tick on each one
when I'd used it. Quite an impressive Nike promotion, I
thought. The only downside to the tick system, well known
among the new breastfeeders of the world, is that when the
milk spurts everywhere or the baby is sick, you end up with
blue rivulets trickling down your chest and puddling in your
cavernous belly button.

The above scenario not quite what you fancy? Let's try
another one, a few weeks later: we spent half of our dispos-
able income on bottles and formula only to have it spewed
back into my hair. After a few stilted conversations with
breastfeeding acquaintances I started to believe the horror
stories about bottle-fed babies ending up with poor development. It'll all be my fault because I didn't exclusively breastfeed him until he was two. I cheered myself up by explaining
to friends the mathematical concept of a number to the
power of 100. Easy, peasy. The squared cm of baby vomit has
about the relative spew stench of the cm coverage x 100.

Are the first few weeks really this bad?

Well, yes and no. The first six weeks are notorious for being
one big wake-up call. Worries and difficulties occasionally
end up way out of proportion, as the above scenarios show.
Forewarned is forearmed in the land of motherhood. So how
would it be if you and I took a sneak preview of the first six

weeks, and scouted out what other women have come up against?

Baby blues

Should the infamous "baby blues" kick in around the third day, then you'll find that your overwhelming tiredness takes second place to the even more overwhelming desire to cry at everything. Rather like those hormonal early weeks of pregnancy, only this time you don't just *feel* like crying, you find yourself actually sobbing at the slightest thing. Lambs in a field, running out of tea bags, heavy boobs, that sort of thing. This phase usually passes after a couple of days, and tiredness will reclaim that number one spot again. Should you find yourself in the depths of despair during those early days, here's a piece of wise advice I had from a lovely midwife with boobs even bigger than mine. She caught me mid-sob when I thought I was on my own in the room. "Oh, sweetheart, what is the matter?" she cooed as I buried my head in her ample bosom. "I shouldn't be feeling so sad when I've got a lovely baby. I think I'm a bad mother already," I confessed as I came up for air. "Oh, chicken. It's just your hormones all of a tizz. It's quite normal to feel like this in the early days. Just have a good cry, girl, let it all out. You'll soon feel better." You know what? She was absolutely right.

What if an aftertaste of this panicky/low feeling lasts longer than a couple of days? For many women, especially those who didn't have their "ideal" birth, it can take weeks before they feel on an emotional even keel again. I found talking about the birth with an understanding friend made a real difference; debriefing, as it were. I even kept a journal in those early weeks, to come to grips with my rampant emotions.

What if a panicky, low feeling lingers for longer than a

couple of weeks? A touch of post-natal depression is possible, regardless of birth experience. A friend of mine had post-natal depression with her first child (she now has five gorgeous kids). Her husband thought she was just overtired but she knew deep down that she didn't feel quite right, so she saw her doctor. She said it was a bit of a shock to be told that she had depression, although it was such a relief to know what the problem actually was. She came through it a month or two later, and used the support offered by her doctor whenever she felt she needed it. She says that she wished she had seen her doctor earlier, because recognising that something was wrong was a real turning point for her.

Afterpains

Don't be fooled into thinking that labour pains finish when the baby is born! They go on happily grinding away for a couple of days, supposedly getting your womb back into shape. All you can do is grit your teeth and chant "hipsters, hipsters" through every grimace. Just don't be a martyr when it comes to pain relief.

Tummy, bum and boobs

Should you be daft enough to look in the mirror, you may notice that the gravity fairy has paid you a surprise visit. Who cares that your womb is supposedly shrinking at an alarming rate, when everything else is lagging behind. Lagging? Sagging? Same difference.

Yes, there's more...

Rocket boobs

The other thing they don't always tell you at antenatal classes is what it's actually like when your milk comes in, the third day after birth. My boobs were like hot, rock hard balloons that you could fry an egg on. I suppose I should have been thrilled at their sheer pertness: two footballs ready for action. I had never seen anything like it; I swear they nearly drilled holes in my T-shirt. The only downside was that they felt full-to-bursting, and they hurt. I think "engorged" is the official term. But, should the titty fairy visit you in this way and they're just too full for comfort, here's the answer.

Express a bit of milk out with your thumb and forefinger (get a midwife to help if you're not sure how) then FEED THE BABY. Relief, joy and bliss as the pressure is relieved. Oh, yes. Even better than a smoothie, and you know what *they're* as good as (see Chapter 1).

Colic

If a baby gets trapped wind with tummy pains, it is said to have colic. Symptoms? Baby screams or grizzles after a feed. No one really seems to know why some babies get it and some don't, or even why it is especially worse in the evenings. The good news is that it usually passes after twelve weeks or so. I don't even know where to start on this one, because for anyone with a baby that is going through it, neat little hints and tips on managing colic are barely more than a cursory glance at something that for some mothers is the final straw.

If you suspect your baby might be colicky, see your health visitor and/or doctor to confirm it and rule out any other problem that may cause similar symptoms, e.g. gastric reflux or allergy. The doctor may want to weigh your baby regularly, and keep a check on his or her general health.

If your baby does suffer from colic you will need your family and friends to support you and give you a break. This is not the time for politeness on your part when someone offers to help you out. "Yes please" is the answer you're looking for. Even though my little Sam was screaming most of the time, I still went to mother and toddler groups, invited friends round and went to the shops. Sometimes I just wanted to shut the rest of the world out I was so shattered. However, deep down I knew that if I was going to cope with the screaming and not lose the plot myself, I needed to still be attached to the rest of the world.

There are plenty of anti-colic medications available, so under the advice of your doctor or pharmacist I'd encourage you to try one or two, as they can be really effective.

OK, so the blues/afterpains/colic/rocket boobs combination doesn't look like a bundle of laughs...

Panic not

- Forewarned is forearmed, and nothing seems quite so bad when it doesn't take you by surprise
- The "six-week combination" is common to (nearly) every new mum. SO, should the occasional blues/rocket-boobs moment head your way, you can smile at yourself secretly as you're wearing the badge of a real mum.

Your body has worked hard for nine months to grow this baby; it is a friend, not the enemy! Things will get better.

Intimate, raw, magical, overwhelming days are to be

found in the early weeks, there is no doubt. I think I prayed more in those weeks than in any time during my pregnancy. Often out of desperation and sheer tiredness. I also found myself praying so much because being with my baby was so amazing that I wanted to hold every moment captive, and share it with our Father God.

I know for certain that a sense of ease rather than unease, a sense of calm rather than stress are actually in the new-mother blessing pack, should you choose to share the weight of the six-week combination with your Father God. On the days when I struggled, I ran to Father God and buried my head just like I did with that lovely midwife. Peace again.

Expectations

Part of the knack of successfully negotiating the first few weeks is not to have unrealistically high expectations of things. If you find yourself with the tiredness/boobs/blues mixture in your lap it's still a pain, but it doesn't get quite the same grip on your psyche as it does when you thought things would be easy once the baby was born. It's worth trying to put any difficulties in the "It won't last forever" department in your head rather than the "I can't do this any more" department. Same problem, just handled differently.

Christian women, on the whole, have crazily high expectations for their mothering, marriage and family life. These things are a big deal to us; we know it matters to get it right. Where we go wrong is that we think that being a Christian means we have to be supermum. We expect to be an ever-patient saint, who whips up a mean casserole and is still good in bed. The result of the unrealistic expectations we place on ourselves is crippling guilt when we feel that we haven't got it right. Guilt, in my opinion is the NUMBER-ONE enemy for all mums. I'm not talking about having a sharp conscience here; of course it is good to weigh our actions and deeds against God's word. What I'm talking about is that nagging "I'm no good at this" niggle that refuses to let up. Maybe what we really need to grasp is that the reality of being a Christian mum is nothing to do with being the perfect mum. It's just about going to God for your pit stops, and allowing him to refresh and fill you and take away the fear. I think it's also about rooting your motherhood in who God says you are, rather than in the day-to-day hurly-burly of your new-mum experience.

The world can wait

Maybe we should all do ourselves a favour and put all our expectations on the shelf for a while, and just enjoy each day. Blasting through motherhood aiming for perfection without pausing to catch your breath is the sure-fire way to get burnout. God loves you just as you are. He will give you the tools you need to bring up your kids. The bumper sticker that says "Let go and let God" is indeed corny, but also not a bad idea. The world is spinning with pressures, expectations and dreams of a better life. It's a rat race, and it gets you nowhere. Just love your God, your husband and your baby with all your heart. Your energy is precious; the world can wait.

"Don't be so busy jumping the waves that you miss the sunset."

Your needs count as important, too!

Another problem with having crazily high expectations in the early weeks is that you could find yourself being so busy try-ing to be perfect that you forget to give yourself a break.

Sometimes the baby WILL HAVE TO WAIT while you finish your meal/have a shower/answer the phone. Just imagine life a few months down the line if you don't set any boundaries at this stage...

You and your husband are having fun in bed (yes, it will actually happen again) and you'll be stopping at five-minute intervals to make pumpkin puree, or shuffle to the kitchen to reload the tumble dryer...

If you don't count your needs as important, too, you'll NEVER DRINK A HOT CUP OF COFFEE AGAIN. You'll go for hours before you realise that your right nipple is poking out of your "easy-feed" shirt with flip-up pockets. I did. The pizza-delivery guy got a tip he hadn't bargained for. My husband's eyes were on stalks when he got home from work.

Have you seen what *she's* doing?

I'm sure it's no surprise to you that there's a bit of a tendency among pregnant/new mums to do a fair bit of comparing with each other, checking out the competition, as it were. If we're honest, a fair bit of criticising goes on as well. If something works well for us, we assume it must be the only right way to do things. So if we bump into another pregnant mum and find out that she's planning to do things differently from us, or going/not going back to work, we immediately make a judgement about that person. Do we have the right to secretly criticise another mum because she's approaching motherhood a little differently? Go too far down this road and we lose our graciousness and respect for one another. Can we really expect God to bless us when we're rampantly criticising others?

He has showed you, O man, what is good. And what does the LORD require of you? To act justly and to love mercy and to walk humbly with your God (Micah 6:8).

Just you and me, kid

When I was pregnant, I remember looking in amazement at a mum who could feed her baby, cuddle her toddler and eat a cinnamon bagel at the same time. Nevertheless, it was amazing how quickly I got used to plonking him over my shoulder or on my hip as I shuffled around. His dad, however, was secretly scared of not supporting our baby's little noggin properly and breaking his neck. He said he was quite comfortable, albeit motionless and rigid, holding the baby only on the high-backed armchair. Eventually pins and needles kicked in, so he valiantly progressed to standing for a few moments with the baby at arms' length. After a few weeks of this he lost all inhibitions and became quite the expert, claiming the sole right to get him back to sleep successfully with a rocking/jigging action that I never even attempted to match. Eventually the baby-rocking master went back to work, I think secretly jealous that he couldn't continue his new-found craft of baby-jigging. He was well on the way to developing the "triple shimmy with a twist" as an ideal solution to a touch of colic.

Pecan and lime purée

So I was now the full-time mum of a real live baby. What if I wanted to go to the loo? What if I slept through a feed? What if I couldn't do it? OK, so I had half a dozen baby manuals informing me how to whip up a mean pecan and lime purée, or how to do origami with a terry nappy. I even had a book on how to use sign language with babies (I got quite into this one until the Greek lady across the road thought I was making obscene gestures). I had books with diagrams on everything from how to bath a baby to what toys to give him at three-month increments.

Next to the book on the rhythm method (never read that one) was a glossy photographic book depicting family life around the world. I was the first to admit that I wasn't particularly photographically cultured; the closest I got to appreciating the art of photography was trooping down to the Athena shop with my brother when I was a teenager. I chose the "bare-chested hunk cradles tiny baby" poster, and he came out clutching the "tennis player scratches her bare bottom" one. I suppose I wasn't heading for great things in the appreciation of photographic art. Well, I figured that as I was at home all day, I should keep an appreciation of culture alive. After all, I'd got 20 minutes to kill before Jerry Springer was on.

I leafed through the black-and-white shots of toothless Mexican women in raucous laughter, and pictures of father and son in cowboy hats tucking in to corn-on-the-cob. I chuckled at the pictures of naked toddlers bathing in an Amazonian stream, and smiled at the mothers breastfeeding as they traded on market stalls in Africa. Suddenly, from nowhere, something finally made sense to me. It sort of clicked that being a good mum is not just about providing exactly the right toy for a four-week-old, then an eight-week-old, and so on. It doesn't really matter whether I can whip up a mean lime purée or not. Being a good mum has nothing to do with whether my baby bathes in an Amazonian stream or a "Winnie the Pooh" bath unit. From the toothless Inuit baby cocooned in fur to the sleeping African baby in her mother's sling, there is one thing they need from their mothers. Is the answer love? Well partly, although the sad fact is that some parents do love their child and yet the child is still neglected emotionally. I think it goes deeper: what your child will need from you as much as love is acceptance. A complete assurance that you are proud of him, without his having to earn your acceptance. This is what all children need.

What babies really need

One night, a few weeks after my second baby was born, I remember having only two hours' sleep. He had colic, I had cracked nipples, and we were both utterly exhausted. As the sun rose he finally dropped off to sleep but I knew I had to get up as I had a doctor's appointment. I turned and looked at my sleeping baby, feeling absolutely spent, with nothing left to give. However, I distinctly remember taking him (asleep) out of the cot and lying him on my chest. No gushing emotions followed as he slept and I dozed. However, that moment was really significant to me because I made a conscious choice TO ACCEPT my baby regardless of my fickle emotions, regardless of whether things would work out as I wanted them to, and of whether he would appreciate me or not. Yes, I still had days when I felt that I got it all wrong, and I still do. Regardless of those feelings, though, I still choose to nurture and cherish my babies, something so much more than keeping them warm and fed. How does nestling and cherishing, and skin-to-skin contact, make your baby feel? It makes him feel safe, accepted. A baby who is held at arms' length will miss out.

I realised one day while I was snuggling up with my baby Samuel that I was craving the same sense of safety for myself. So I spent some time looking at this verse...

I will take refuge in the shadow of your wings... (Psalm 57:1).

The image portrayed here is that even the mere shadow of the wing brings relief and security. Sometimes the demands and strains of the early weeks can feel like toiling in a desert under constant blazing heat. The early weeks are intense; each moment is new and exhilaration often walks hand in hand with despair. I longed for someone to tell me it was all OK, and take the strain for a little while. Someone to bring a cool breeze to the hot, weary nights. Psalm 57:1 was my answer to the incessant effort of the early weeks. As I nestled, cuddled and protected my little one, so I came to the Father and nestled myself in him. I just told him everything that I felt, just as it was. At last I felt safe. I felt refreshed so that I could give again. And so the cycle continued; I'd stock up on peace and strength from God so that I could give it out to my family. I'm still in that cycle now. I've just stumbled upon a wisdom nugget that taught me that to nurture my babies: I must allow myself to be nurtured first. On the days when I don't do this I end up running out of steam. He is my breath, my warmth, my extra blanket in the night. I can't do motherhood without him.

Time out with your Father God

What do you think is the greatest gift a pregnant mum could receive from God?

Protection from harm?
Strength to give birth?
Blessing for her baby?
Fear to be taken away?

Good health?
Food and a safe house?

There are many needs at this crucial time in life and the Father hears our every cry. However, there is one need that I believe is greater than all the others on the list. It is simply the gift of the Father's kiss. Knowing God as Father.

This is something of which it is all too easy to have head-knowledge rather than real experience. A while ago I found myself concluding that God just put up with me. I remember thinking, "I mess up! All the time! How can the Holy of holies actually want anything more than to just put up with me?" The answer, I've since discovered, is grace. I used to think that grace was God forgiving our sins. Of course it is partly this, but the forgiveness of sins is only the tip of the iceberg as far as God's grace is concerned. The point is that God's grace stretches so wide that he is longing for us at the very moment when we are at our very worst. He doesn't just put up with us, he passionately loves us as we are. That's a Father's love.

The story of the prodigal son describes the father preparing a feast, getting out the finest robes and throwing a party because his failed and filthy child has returned to him. The Father's kiss, the Father's embrace. We cannot earn it. All we can do is run into his arms and know that we are loved and lovely in the eyes of Almighty God.

Chapter 10 Feeding Babies (What the Leaflets Don't Tell You)

I had a cunning plan. I'd heard that life with a new baby could be frenetic, so I devised a strategy to cancel out any chaos that the early weeks might throw at me. My expert plan? Well, I carefully drew up a list of everything that I wanted to do in an average day, including looking after the baby's needs. There it was, all neatly written out, and all I had to do was to manage these ten things a day. Feeding the baby was slotted in at regular intervals. Ten ticks, and domestic bliss would be mine! Here is the masterpiece:

1. Feed baby.
2. Get dressed.
3. Tidy up.
4. Feed baby, etc.
5. Get lunch.
6. Do laundry.
7. GO OUT SOMEWHERE!
8. Prepare/eat evening meal.
9. Feed baby, etc.
10. Bath and bed.

Just one thing I hadn't banked on. My baby had other ideas. First he staked his claim on me by snuggling his downy little head into my neck. I was hooked. Next he took rather a liking to feeding. So much so, that I rarely reached "step two" by noon. It is safe to say that whatever a pregnant mum THINKS it will be like to feed a baby, it is never quite how she imagined it.

The whole business of feeding babies has reached dizzy heights in the crazy world of parenting "hot potatoes". Opinions run high on how, what and when to feed a newborn baby. Fortunately, with or without a cunning plan, successful feeding is absolutely achievable.

Ode to breastfeeding

Now this wouldn't be a pregnancy book worth reading if it didn't give a whistle-stop tour of breastfeeding. So here follow some hot tips on breastfeeding (for want of a better phrase!). And guess what? It's another list of ten!

Top ten reasons to breastfeed your baby
 1. It contains all the nutrients and water your baby needs.
 2. It reduces the risk of infections and allergies during childhood.
 3. It reduces the cancer risk for mum.
 4. It's a unique bonding experience.
 5. It's free.
 6. It burns up mum's spare calories, which means you lose that "baby belly" more quickly.
 7. You don't have the hassle of buying/preparing formula and sterilising bottles.
 8. Once you get used to it, you can feed anywhere. Your life does not revolve around "feed times".

9. The milk adapts to the baby's needs as she grows.
10. It's a brilliant, quick comforter for an unsettled baby – night or day.

A list of ten is all well and good. Most of us have heard it before, and we've also heard how difficult breastfeeding can be. So, tempting as it is to stay cosily in the lists of ten, how about us taking a look at the real day-to-day business of feeding babies...

Breast or bottle?

Some pregnant mums I have met who are considering bottle-feeding are doing so purely because they have silent doubts about breastfeeding.

WHAT IF... I can't do it?
WHAT IF... I have to go back to work?
WHAT IF... I have to get my boobs out in public?
WHAT IF... My breasts/nipples are too big/small?

Later in the chapter we'll look at these concerns. But for now let's look at the phrase WHAT IF...

If we lived by the WHAT IF school of thought, we would never do anything new or even a teensy bit challenging. We'd never get married, make friends, and have babies. Life would be dull, dull, dull. OK, so breastfeeding is a huge step into unknown territory; the WHAT IF worries are clamouring for attention. Well I've got a WHAT IF of my own for you...

WHAT IF YOU GIVE BREASTFEEDING A TRY? YOU DON'T LOSE ANYTHING BY TRYING. IT MIGHT BE ONE OF THE BEST THINGS YOU'VE EVER DONE. WHAT IF THE "WHAT IF'S" DIDN'T CALL THE SHOTS ANY MORE?

The *Dear Lord, I Feel Like a Whale!* guide to breastfeeding

How hard can it be? Baby opens mouth. Mother puts nipple in baby's mouth. Baby guzzles away merrily. What's the big deal? I thought that I knew all about it – I'd read the "breast is best" chapter in my baby manual from start to end. Breastfeeding buzzwords like "empowered", "natural", "bonding", "easy", laced the text like fresh cream on a strawberry pavlova. Is breastfeeding really the delicious garden party of delights the manuals would suggest? The good news is that breastfeeding *can* be a strawberry pavlova in the paltry diet that can be the experience of the first few weeks. To eat pavlova you need spoons; without spoons you've got no chance...

The silver spoons of breastfeeding

Silver spoon 1: Position

- Get comfortable. If you're sitting, make sure you are upright and your lap is almost flat. If you are lying down, lie fairly flat, with a pillow under your head. Try and lie well over onto your side. Don't have the whole weight of the baby in your arms, or they will get tired and drag down during the feed. Have a cushion on your lap to help support her, or let the bed take her weight when you are lying down
- Have the baby's whole body facing you with her head, shoulders, and body in a straight line
- Her nose should be lined up with your nipple, her body close so she doesn't have to stretch to reach the breast
- Have one hand under her head ready to guide her onto the nipple. Use the other hand to support and guide your

breast. Support the whole breast, not just the nipple, with your fingers underneath and your thumb on top.

Silver spoon 2: Latching on

- Touch her lips gently with your nipple until she opens her mouth really wide
- Use your hand that is supporting her head to quickly move her onto the breast, the moment her mouth is open really wide
- What you are aiming for at this point is the baby getting a big mouthful of breast, not just chomping on the nipple. That's why it's called breastfeeding, not nipple-feeding! If she's on correctly her chin will be touching the breast, and her sucking pattern will quickly change from short sucks to long, deep sucks
- Here's a useful tip for latching on: using the thumb on the hand that is supporting the breast, push down on the areola bit just above the nipple as the baby is about to latch on. This points the nipple upwards and may help it reach the top, back part of the baby's mouth.

Silver spoon 3: Feed often

- Newborn babies have tiny tummies and will need feeding often. Go with their demands, they will soon settle into a routine after a few weeks
- Breastfeeding works on a demand-and-supply system: the more you let her feed, the more milk you will produce.

Breastfeeding is a rare and beautiful thing, most definitely worth the effort. Unfortunately, breastfeeding doesn't always work out as expected. Forget the pavlova – breastfeeding when it's not going well is utterly grim; more of a fish-soup experience. If this is you, and you've picked this up for a smidgen of advice before your nipples fall off, you've come to the right place.

Who stole my pavlova?

Breastfeeding problems, why they happen and what to do

He wants to feed all the time. What if my milk isn't enough for him?

It is absolutely normal for babies to feed really frequently during the first few weeks. Each time your baby feeds, the milk supply is being built up. This is the time to hang on in there, and trust your body to do one of the jobs it was designed for. Your baby won't be this demanding forever. Try and keep the baby near you as much as possible, and let feeding become a normal part of a cuddle with him rather than the "big deal" of "feeding time". I'd definitely recommend having the baby in your room at night. You barely have to wake up to feed him, and he will feel safe and secure.

Feeding her is excruciating. My nipples are cracked and bleeding. I can't do this any more.

(Lucy, 32)

There are some things that are impossible to put into words. It's impossible to describe the smell of a wet cat, it's impossible to describe the sound of chalk on a blackboard. It is absolutely impossible to put into words the pain of cracked nipples. There is no pain quite like this one; you never forget it. My eyes on stalks, teeth bared, my toes curling, and that was just at the thought of feeding. I also remember the moment when it stopped, just like that. I had contacted La Leche League, at my wits' end. They explained very clearly that sore nipples are due to the baby not latching on properly. They explained all about positioning (see Spoon 1). I had heard it all before, but at this stage I would have tried anything. So I completely changed my feeding position and tried a different one that they recommended. I held him like a bowling ball under my arm, with his little feet poking out behind me. I carefully made sure I followed the steps you'll find in Spoons 1 and 2. It worked.

My boobs are drilling holes in my T-shirt.
(engorgement and mastitis)

Never in my life would I have thought that I would be the proud owner of what must have been a 36FF chest. Firm, pert. Now here was a bonus of having babies that you don't hear about. Just one problem: they started to get so full, they hurt. It was like the day my milk came in (day three) revisited, only this time I didn't know why. "The return of the mammaries", "the attack of the footballs", call it what you like. By the evening they were like water balloons ready to burst. By midnight I was mumbling guttural words, and they weren't tongues. By 7am I was on the phone to the on-call midwife, begging her for help, or at least the number of the nearest cosmetic surgeon who would willingly take a pair of 36GGG off my hands.

The answer to my dilemma came by the covert action of my bra, as I tried in vain to stuff my GGGs into a C-cup so I looked presentable if the midwife came round. The jostling and fumbling it took to stuff my boobs in was no mean feat, with the knock-on effect of them leaking milk. All the squashing and fumbling made them spurt everywhere, leaking in rivulets down my jeans. After a while they were soft enough for me to actually latch on my near-ravenous baby, who completed the job nicely. Hallelujah (and I meant it). I was quite chuffed by my secret discovery of how to sort the problem of engorged boobs; I felt like a breastfeeding pioneer. Maybe I should patent my method and manufacture twee gingham bras with built-in drawstrings to tighten things up and squash out the milk. I was quite disappointed to be informed by the midwife that getting the milk out yourself is called expressing, and it's been done practically since the dawn of time. That's my patent out of the window, then. And I thought breast pumps were just for when you wanted to stash some in the freezer.

Mastitis involved all of the above symptoms, and you also feel hot, feverish and not very well. It doesn't mean the end of breastfeeding, but you definitely need to visit your doctor, because you might need antibiotics to sort the infection out. In the meantime, feed your baby as normal.

I just can't do this any more...
(when it seems that breastfeeding is not going to work for you)

There is nothing worse when your nipples are hanging off than being given patronising little one-liners such as "no one said being a mum was easy", or "you'll get there in the end". You've got the no-sleep-and-cracked-nipples combo, and the game just ain't fun no more. May I suggest two pit stops before you throw in the towel?

1) Get good advice
Request a home visit from a breastfeeding counsellor, your midwife or your health visitor; someone who knows what they are doing and can help you latch on correctly.

2) Get support
If you're going to beat this problem you need to recharge. Insist that you sleep when the baby does. Get help from your husband at night, yes, even if he has to work the next day. Don't even attempt to do anything else for a few days; you have to rest if you're going to recharge. Enlist the mother-in-law in a few baby-rocking duties while you catnap. Make it happen, girl!

I still can't do this any more...

So, what if you've tried everything you can, and the breast-feeding business is not for you? There may be a medical reason why you can't breastfeed (although these are pretty rare). You may have simply chosen to bottle-feed from the word go...

Some of us reading this will bottle-feed. Some out of personal choice, some as a last resort. Having successfully bottle-fed baby number one, then successfully breastfed baby number two (for a couple of years), I'd like to make a point here. How you feed your baby does not dictate your "rating" as a mother, as some would have us believe. OK, you could argue that breastfeeding has better health and psychological benefits. There is no doubt that it is the better choice all round. But somehow life's choices aren't always as black and white as we would like, and other factors come into play, such as bleeding nipples, or no proper teaching on how to latch on, or being on drugs that aren't compatible with breastfeeding. There are no "grade 1" mothers and "grade 2" mothers purely on the basis of what milk a baby is receiving. You either are a mother or you're not. Each of us weaves our numerous threads of mothering choices throughout the years, thus creating unique pictures. WHAT you feed your baby is not so much of an issue as HOW you feed your baby (more on this in a minute!).

But first, a special note to those feeling like a Feeding Failure.

This is a lonely place to be. If your feeding plans don't work out as intended, you might find yourself with a mixture of disappointment and frustration rampantly trashing any shred of pleasure at being a mum. Remember, the milk you feed your baby does not have to dictate your mothering. It's just milk. Has your love changed for your baby? NO. We will all have regrets or come across difficulties in our parenting journey. It's a bumpy road sometimes. Pick yourself up, dust yourself down and give yourself a treat. After all, you're a mum now. Then you should go full-throttle at nurturing and cherishing your baby. Make tomorrow a fresh start and have a snugglefest with your little bundle.

Here is a fridge-ministry slot especially for you. Copy it out and stick it on your fridge!

Lift up your head, you are not alone. I am the Lord of the seasons, the seas, the skies. I know when an autumn leaf falls, when a fish leaps, when the dew will form. I know you. I know your hopes and dreams, the cries of your heart. I know your seasons of searing heat, dry and crumpled. I am the Lord of the seasons. Come to me my child, I will refresh you and show you the way. Then, you will dance in the rain.

(Anonymous)

Pause, focus, cherish, feed

Stoke up your sardine smoothie again, because I'm going to say something really radical and suggest that there are bigger fishes in the sea of parenthood than what you feed your baby. In your own little world at home, with everyone else's opinions shut out, feeding is what you make it. I really encourage you to make it a big deal, but in a new way, just for the two of you. Whether you end up breastfeeding or bottle-feeding, make it super-special, one-to-one time. Even if you have a carpet-biting toddler/demanding lifestyle/never-ending list of things to do. Pause, focus, cherish and feed. Discipline yourself to give quality cuddles, not snatched moments. Cherishing comes from the heart, not a nipple or a teat.

When baby number two (Samuel) came along, my first baby (Joseph) was only just walking (birth control was never our strong point). So the "pause, focus, cherish, feed" took on a whole new dimension with a rampant toddler to contend with. Especially as this time I was breastfeeding properly for the first time. I tried to make feeding a snugglefest for all of us and told them both how precious they were. The ambience was often broken by Joseph wandering off to lick the fish tank, or trying to post biscuits into my bra.

It was during one of those wriggly, cuddly feeding sessions that I suddenly felt that God gave me a "word". Now I wouldn't class myself as the type to "have a word from the Lord" as I'm mowing the lawn or defrosting the fridge. I look in awe at people who do, as when I'm doing chores I'm more likely to be wondering if I can get away with not doing my roots for one more week, or working out how many weeks until Christmas.

Enclave

Anyway, there I was being mummy, and a word was burning into my heart, soul and head. "Enclave". Nothing else, just "enclave". The only problem was, I'd never heard of this word before. I wondered if it was my subconscious requesting a glass of wine; "enclave" sounded suspiciously like a Portuguese red to me. I've not got this "getting a word" bit 100% nailed, so I threw what I felt God was saying at the Bible to see if it stood true or not. As it happens, I discovered that an enclave is...

> A garden... a spring enclosed, a sealed fountain (Song of Songs 4:12).

Intrigued? I was. I found out that most of the gardens in Old-Testament times were open to anyone who happened to be passing. Even animals could come and drink from their flowing springs and fountains. However, the gates in an enclave garden weren't ajar for strangers and animals to wander in. An enclave was for the delight of the king. It was a garden where his invited guests could be refreshed by its stunning beauty, with the overpowering fragrance of thousands of flowers caressing their senses.

So what relevance does "enclave" have to a young mum feeding a baby, a mum who was never any good at gardening anyway?

I believe God was speaking to me about the cherishing moments of feeding time. A time when the baby is welcome to drink in love and nourishment. She does not drink from any passing fountain. Feeding time is intimate time, one to one. She delights in her mummy and her mummy delights in her. The King of kings delights in both mother and baby, and adorns them with flowers of his blessing. I'm so mesmerised by this image of family cuddles being such an intimate time of blessing that we have named our house "Enclave". Soon my baby-feeding days will be over (if we get our act together on the birth-control front). But hopefully we'll have built a routine of giving cherish moments, pausing to delight in each other, receiving the blessing of the King of kings.

Oops, I did it again!

Owing to the blood-pressure medication I am currently on, I won't be able to breastfeed long-term when this baby is born, although I intend to try for as long as possible. I'm determined that, whatever milk my little one is receiving, he or she will receive my best cherishing. However, I can guarantee that as soon as I start whipping out a bottle, other mothers will make a silent judgement about my mothering, my lifestyle, and probably my upbringing while they're at it. Outrageous!

Checking out the competition

The world we live in now often feels like a rat race where everyone's chasing to get ahead of one another. This rubs off on parenthood too; we measure ourselves against others, checking out the competition. We don't mean to do it; it just sort of happens – a lot. Now here's a question for you: why are mothers renowned for gossiping the world over? Maybe it is because we don't want to fail our own brood, so we make ourselves feel better by having a go at others, silently or out loud. Maybe we just can't resist gossiping.

I'm not that happy. Breastfeeding is harder than I thought and everyone is so interested in my baby. It's like I don't exist any more.

I'm struggling to connect with my baby, Alysha. I don't know what's wrong with me. She feeds and sleeps really well so no one at church has thought to ask if I'm OK. They all think I must be happy because she is an easy baby.

No one talked to me at toddler group after I gave up breast-feeding. It was as if I didn't have anything of interest to say any more. They wrote me off. I never went again.

I told my friend that I wasn't really enjoying being a mum. It's because I can't get the birth out of my head. When I do, I know I'll be fine. My friend told people what I said and now half the church thinks I can't cut it as a mother. I just want to crawl away and hide.

You see the common thread running through these real-life examples? It's the discouragement that kicks in when another mother does not care. New mums are not islands: we bump into each other at parks; we talk at nurseries; we chat at church and at baby clinics. So how about commiting our-selves to being encouragers, rather than discouragers? How about choosing not to judge, but to lift up instead? What a different place toddler group would be if no one commented on anyone else, not even silently. Dare we even think that the impact could go as far as our babies' generation being less judgemental than our own? Mothers are world-shapers, so let's shape beautifully. Let's not tear down what God is raising up.

Time out with your Father God

Dear Lord,

You breathed on me and gave me life. Without you, I am nothing. With you, I am more than I ever could imagine. Thank you for accepting me, just as I am. Please help me to give the same acceptance and unconditional love to my loved ones. Show me how to love, how to nurture, and how to cherish. Show me how to make nurturing my baby a priority. Soften my heart that I might serve you all the days of my life.

Amen.

Chapter 11   # "It's Not Supposed to Be Like This!"

I used to be a real sucker for TV adverts. My favourite one was the "cute romping baby meets playful puppy in cornfield". I even liked the "muscle-bound hero rescues stranded blonde from top of waterfall" one. When I was pregnant I was even worse, sobbing at the one where the tiny baby clings on to her mother's back as she hangs the white billowing washing out. That was then. Now? Well, I'm a hardened consumer who dashes out for a skinny latte during the break like the rest of the world. Why the rebuff? Does the cute toddler in the hay bales not do it for me any more? Not even the sleeping baby in a super-white baby vest? No. Well, after a few years of marriage, four pregnancies and nearly three children, I've realised something: when it comes to real life, things don't always work out quite in the ideal way. Take, for example, marriage-night sex. Is it always the multi-orgasmic cocktail of delights some marriage courses would have us believe? I rest my case.

We all have daydreams about what it's like to have a baby. Sometimes things don't work out quite as expected, and it can feel as if life is short-changing you. Is motherhood how it looks in the adverts? Sometimes it feels more like a puppy massacre, and the fluffy bunnies won't play any more. It is indeed possible that, at some point, you might find yourself mumbling (yelling?) "It's not supposed to be like this!".

I'm not supposed to feel like a robot, am I?

Let's clear this one up straight away. Tiny babies need loads of attention. They need feeding very often and will wake frequently with hunger, night and day. They will sometimes cry inconsolably for no apparent reason. This is normal for tiny babies. It is the same for every single baby born on the same day as yours. It's what they do.

Therefore, do yourself a favour and expect to feel as if you're on autopilot for the first few weeks. Anything more will then be a bonus. Don't give yourself grief over your lack of freedom. It's how it is for everyone. Although it's impossible to realise when you're in it, this phase does not last for ever. Don't resist the sudden change in the focus of your life; ease yourself into it, and before you know it a new norm will emerge and you'll feel a sense of you again.

I'm not supposed to be this tired, am I?

I confess that, before I had kids, tiredness to me meant a hard day at work, a late night or having to get up before 9am on a Saturday. Now, I think that there should be two words for tired. One word for those who have never had children, and another word for those with a baby. "Blaaah" would be good for those who are parents. It's about all you can utter after 48 hours of no sleep, with baby on a milk marathon, and all the relatives arriving in half an hour. The only way out of this one is OBVIOUSLY to get some sleep, but sometimes that seems impossible. If you reach the "blaaah" stage, welcome to the club. But, here's a way out of the club that no one wanted to join in the first place.

Who was the person who rubbed your back during those endless contractions? Who was the one who came with you to the ultrasound scan? Whom would you count as your closest friend? Well, forget the back-rubbing, hand-holding role that they once held. Now is the time you really need them; they are the key to your getting some sleep and sanity. This is your husband/birth partner's chance to take on a "sleep-protector" role for which you will be eternally grateful.

Three steps to (near) sanity

1) Potential visitors should be telephoned and advised that they are very welcome to come and visit the baby, in seven days' time. You have waited nine months for this, and you need to sleep. You'll have plenty of time to catch up with friends/show the baby off/tidy the house when you are rested.

2) Your husband can take on the role of looking after the baby in between feed times. Many mums find it hard to relinquish their mummy role, even to the baby's dad. Let the umbilical cord stretch enough to include a couple of others in the baby's care. If you get some sleep, even if it is just a few catnaps, you'll be able to be the mum you want to be.

3) Don't even think about cooking a meal/tidying up for the first week. That's what takeaways and good friends are for!

A few more ideas...

This is a time to be firm. Everyone and everything is going to have to wait. Bring the baby into your bedroom so that you barely have to wake up to feed her. You'll have plenty of time to establish a cot routine with her in a few weeks when you've caught up on sleep. If you do have to get up to feed, don't turn on the lights or chatter to the baby. With any luck, if she's not stirred too much, she'll drift back off to sleep. Similarly, unless her nappy is soiled or very wet, don't change it until the morning.

Some mums camp out in the bedroom for the first few days. This certainly makes it easier to nap between feeds, although it is important that new mums take gentle exercise each day, as this will help you to recover better.

Even the creator of heaven and earth needed to rest...

> By the seventh day God had finished the work he had been doing; so on the seventh day he rested from all his work (Genesis 2:2).

I'm not supposed to be utterly burnt out, am I?

Five days after a C-section I congratulated myself on how well I was doing as I humped the vacuum cleaner up the stairs. Three days later I was whizzing round to my friends' houses, baby and toddler in tow, showing off my baby. In the evenings I stayed up as late as the rest of the adult world as I didn't want to "miss out" (on what I'm still not sure). And so I carried on "getting the most out of life". The more my whirlwind of activity continued, the less I felt able to relax, so the more I did. Activity became the security blanket that I hid my insecurities under. The only problem was, the supermum train was going to just one place, burnout city. I was exhausted, and breastfeeding was becoming difficult. I then discovered for myself the following truth, that burnt-out mums will find their hearts broken when they realise that, in all their activity, they have forgotten the treasure of simply being a mum. I had been so busy. What did I have to show for it? I thought that I was living life to the full, but I was fooling myself. Stop the supermum train! I want to get off!

Stop the supermum train, I want to get off!

I got off the supermum train by going to the park for a whole day, just me and my baby. We fed the ducks and I prayed. I told God about how my busy life was consuming me. He listened. I told him how I was kind of scared that if I slowed the pace down, I might find out that I'm not actually a very good mum. I told him that I was also desperately trying to hold on to a sense of "me". He listened. I had a little cry sitting next to a tree as my baby slept. He comforted me as if I were his baby. I rummaged in my rucksack for my pocket Bible, covered in biscuit crumbs. I read about a tree that sank its roots into clear water and grew tall and strong, like an oak tree. I asked him for some living water for my soul. I said I was sorry for trying to live without his water. He filled me up again. I changed my baby's nappy. He filled me up a bit more. I went home and stuck this on my fridge and engraved it on my heart. I was happy again.

> But blessed is the man who trusts in the LORD, whose confidence is in him. He will be like a tree planted by the water that sends out its roots by the stream. It does not fear when heat comes; its leaves are always green. It has no worries in a year of drought and never fails to bear fruit (Jeremiah 17:7–8).

That was a few years ago, but I have no intention of getting on the supermum train again. Now I try not to let the insignificant busyness of life consume all of my attention. It's just not worth it! And I remember the tree.

I don't know what I'm doing

There's not a mum I know who hasn't at some time silently felt that she hasn't a clue what she's doing, at some stage or another. There is no easy path of parenthood that guarantees success; it can be a bumpy ride. In the early days it's easy to feel a failure simply because everything from feeding to pushing a pram is new and uncertain. However, unfamiliarity doesn't mean you're doing anything wrong. You and your baby are both getting to know each other, and confidence comes as you get more practice. Support from health professionals is a real confidence-booster, and a safety net should you need further support. They will also check your baby's weight gain and general health regularly, so that you can be reassured and advised where necessary. This is not the time to keep worries to yourself, as new mums often have many worries in common and your health professional may have just the right answer for you. Meeting up with other new mums can be a real help as you share trials and triumphs.

I feel so stressed!

Having a baby is one of those "significant life events" that can trigger all sorts of coping mechanisms to deal with the stress. Some of us have better ways of dealing with stress than others. Going for a run is supposed to be one of the best ways of relieving stress. If anyone can prise me away from the fridge, I might give it a try one day!

Most of the time, stress fades away if the stressful situation is addressed. For example, getting to grips with breast-feeding can be very stressful at the time. Then, as feeding becomes easier, the stress melts away and is replaced by a melted-toffee sense of well-being as you feed. Many problems that occur during the early weeks of life with a baby can be positively resolved; others we may just have to work through. Stress is unquestionably one of the top problems of the early months. I reckon that 80% of chocoholics are new mums! A friend of mine raked up quite a credit-card bill on new shoes after she had a baby. It's no secret that our society offers "crutches" galore.

The problem with crutches

I suspect there could be a problem if one of those "crutches" becomes more permanent. For example, raking up quite a credit-card bill or working through the fridge at an alarming rate, even when the initial new-baby stress has disappeared. Most of these crutches are known only to the person using them, and if we're not careful they can become a guilty secret that won't go away. The early years of parenthood seem to be a prime time for those crutches to take hold – you know the ones: overeating, smoking, overspending, and drinking. Maybe it is because new parents are "on call" 24/7 that we feel that there needs to be some release, a way of feeling better. Having a whole packet of chocolate biscuits to yourself seems an indulgence worthy of the day you've had. I've talked to new mums who've said that, before you know it, these things become more than a distraction or a treat; they become something you can't say no to. Guilt and shame tag along and, before you know it, you've got a precious new mum full of godly potential who now feels bound and gagged by a treat that became a habit.

The obvious answer from the outside is to "get help". However, the sting in the tail of many of these habits is that they are often a secret. I remember a mum who was mortified at the thought of her friends finding out that she smoked ten cigarettes a day. She couldn't think of anything worse. She kept it to herself for many years, a guilty secret.

There are many habits that are truly addictive; smoking and drinking are the biggest culprits. If this is you, may I advise you to join the throng of many mums before you who have gone to their doctor to get proper help. There are all sorts of counselling and support programmes that have proved really effective. There is top-notch support available; just tell your doctor.

So what about the grey area that isn't so talked about in the media? Those with habits that could lead to addiction in the years to come? That's an area in which I think new mums are particularly vulnerable. We're back to that whole pack of chocolate cookies, or the out-of-control spending, or the occasional flirting. I guess the bottom line is this question that we should all consider: Does anything have more of a hold on us than it should do, or does any desire have mastery over us (other than the desire for Jesus himself)? The moment you submit yourself to something that is not of God, you have handed dominion over that area to the enemy of God. Sounds heavy, but it's true. A young mum who loves her God but finds herself giving in to a smoking/drinking/overeating/flirting habit will have left herself spiritually gagged and bound. So many of God's children can be found in this cold and lonely place. So what do you do if a habit has mastery over you? Do you find yourself submitting to the "master" and feeding the desires? It has got to be time to blow the horn and shout freedom to the captives in the name of Jesus. But HOW?

1) Confess that you have messed up. Repenting before God is the first step towards freedom for all of us.
2) Tell someone else. Break the secrecy and get help, be it family support, medical help or pastoral support.

3) Jesus said he had come to set the captives free. Call out to him; resist bad habits, and the old master will run.

> Submit yourselves, then, to God. Resist the devil, and he will flee from you. Come near to God and he will come near to you. Wash your hands, you sinners, and purify your hearts, you double-minded. Grieve, mourn and wail. Change your laughter to mourning and your joy to gloom. Humble yourselves before the Lord, and he will lift you up (James 4:7–10).

Then what will become of the young woman whose gags and blindfolds lie in rags at her feet? Will she stay curled up all alone? No: the true master, Jesus, will pick her up. The master will make her into his masterpiece. He will mould her into someone of great dignity and strength as she remains submitted to him. A masterpiece is a work of the finest quality. The artist takes his time over every detail. The piece is held in high regard and all who see it applaud the artist. There is much of the artist's distinctive character in it. It's beautiful.

> I ... make the dry tree flourish (Ezekiel 17:24).

My baby won't stop crying

There's something about the sound of your baby crying that just stops you in your tracks. Not even sleep is an escape. I could bear a whole class full of snotty toddlers throwing their worst tantrums and I wouldn't bat an eyelid. Even a herd of whingeing nine-year-old girls wouldn't bother me. Nor even rowdy teenagers. Even other people's babies crying sounds like bleating lambs to my ears. My own baby wailing? Well that's a whole different story.

Why do tiny babies cry?

Tiny babies have tiny tummies that empty quickly and need filling often. This is particularly true if you are breast-feeding, as your baby may well cry for food very often while she is building up your milk supply. It can be really tough, but there is no point refusing her food and trying to force her to wait. Feed by demand, even when the demand is great! Routine and set feed times will come naturally as her stomach becomes big enough to hold a little more milk. Hunger is the number-one reason for crying.

What if you've fed her and she is still crying?

Try feeding her again. This doesn't mean that there is anything wrong with your milk. All babies have ravenous phases; remember that they are growing each day. They need the energy supplies. Check that she is latched on properly and swallowing as she sucks.

Still crying?

Check her nappy. Is she too hot or cold? Does she simply need to feel you close to her?

Still crying?

Try feeding her again.

Still crying?

Stress levels start to rise... What if she is ill? Check for the common signs of illness (fever, unresponsiveness, unusual cry, listlessness, rash). If you are in any doubt over her health, take her to see a doctor. Tiny babies are always a high priority in any doctor's workload.

Ten ways to soothe a crying baby

1) Feed her (even if you've only just finished feeding her!)

2) Invest in a baby sling and carry her about with you throughout the day

There is something special about wearing a baby that I can't quite put my finger on. Maybe it's feeling a warm, downy head nestling into you, or maybe it's that sense of closeness that reminds me of when my baby was first born. Whatever it is, baby-carrying is perhaps the most popular method of soothing crying babies the world over. It settles babies like magic. Millions of mums can't be wrong.

While we're on the subject of baby-carriers, take your time in choosing one. Some seem to hang the baby's entire weight around your neck, leaving you feeling like a hunch-back by the end of the day. There are baby-carriers available to wear on your front, back and side. Some have metal frames; most are made from soft material. I had a baby sling, identical in style to those worn in Africa. This style is certainly flexible, as it can be used front, back and side, it doesn't have to be removed for breastfeeding, and it actually gives you a bit of privacy for feeding. It can carry from a newborn up to a five-year-old, and it can just be thrown into the washing machine as often as you need (a crucial point with my messy babies).

3) Keep on the move

Many a dad has driven round and round the block to calm their wailing cherub. Motion, whether it's in the car or the pram, is a sure-fire way to calm most babies down.

4) Fresh air

A wander round the garden carrying your whingeing baby is not so well known but is equally effective in the calming-baby stakes. Maybe it's the motion of the trees swaying, or the whistling of the wind.

5) Music

Hearing a familiar song can be very soothing for little ones. "Somewhere Over the Rainbow" is the lullaby of choice in our household (although I do turn the baby-listening device off when I sing – no need to subject the whole downstairs to my warbling). Having a CD player in the baby's room is a great idea, although no substitute for a mummy's lullaby.

6) Scripture

> When I was heavily pregnant with my daughter, I went to visit my very frail gran. She was fast asleep for the whole time that I was there, so I just sat on her bed and held her hand. I prayed the scripture to her, "May the Lord bless you and keep you. Cause his face to shine upon you, be gracious unto you and give you peace." For a fleeting moment I felt so privileged. There I was, sitting by a gracious woman of God close to her time to going home to heaven. I was also carrying a girl given by God; I had a real sense of God the giver of life. My gran did go home to heaven two weeks later. A few days later, my daughter Miranda Rose was born. I pray that same scripture over her every night as I put her to bed. Now she's nearly two, she knows a few words and says a big AMEN at the end.
>
> (JECB)

Speaking scripture over your baby is one of the best things you can do, whether they are crying or not. You are actively blessing and nourishing their souls. If scripture is part of the normal chatter of the house when your baby is young, it will become a strong foundation for the years to come.

7) Comforter

Little ones have special bonds with their favourite toy or blanket; this bond can be very comforting. I specifically chose comforter toys for my little ones that were safe, soft and not too big or heavy. However, there's no telling whether your little cherub will attach herself to the dog's squeaky toy or a huge fluffy blanket. I have a friend whose toddler simply would not be parted from a huge patchwork quilt his auntie had knitted him. The quilt was filthy from being dragged on the ground, dropped in puddles and trapped in the car door numerous times. In the end his mum had no choice but to cut it into smaller squares. She barely slept that night, imagining her toddler's distraught face as he realised that his blanket had been cut into pieces. She needn't have worried. He came dashing into kitchen with a look of delight on his face: "Look, mummy, blanky's had babies!"

8) Triple shimmy with a twist

I've already mentioned that special baby-jigging role known only to fathers. It's a mystery, but daddies do hold the monopoly on the art of baby-rocking. What can I say? Babies love being rocked by their daddy. Whether daddy will want to do his rocking bit at 3am is a different matter!

9) Soothers/dummies/pacifiers

OK, so I've avoided this hot potato so far. Many of you may already hold strong views on the use of soothers: you may think they are fantastic comforters for fussy babies and sanity-savers for the babies' mums. Or you may hold the view that they damage the chances of successful breastfeeding, and they lead to more wakeful nights as the baby wakes and cries for the dummy instead of going back to sleep. One of my babies had a dummy; one of my babies never had one past his mouth. I'm certainly no expert on this, but I know for certain that dummies are a hindrance rather than a help if you are establishing breastfeeding. There's definitely a point to be made about their effect on bonding. If a tiny baby has a dummy, it becomes far easier just to stick the dummy in rather than give a cuddle, and if that happens frequently, it can't be good. What about an older baby? This one is down to personal choice, like many things on the jungle track of parenthood. Many mums use soothers just at night, so they don't become cuddle-replacers during the day.

10) Feed them again
OK, so I'm cheating! Take note, however: the number-one reason for young babies to cry is that they *need another feed!*

Losing your temper

I was asked by a fellow mum to include this subject in the book. This paragraph is for all of us, however calm we might feel right now. As I said, there is nothing on earth like the sound of your baby screaming the house down. Top that off with a generous helping of sleep deprivation and feeding difficulties, and even the most mild-mannered of us feel the pressure. There's my first point: feeling absolutely frustrated, and past your coping point is more common than many new mothers will admit. The important part is releasing and controlling your emotions in the best way.

If you feel close to snapping

1) Find someone to talk to. Pop round to a neighbour's house, call a friend, ring your mum, call in at the shops. Don't isolate yourself; it only escalates your emotions. The crucial point here is to get support. Your doctor's surgery is certainly worth contacting, as there will be different support options available to you there.

2) Contact a recommended support group for valuable resources and contact with other mums who have gone through the depths of despair and come out the other side.

3) Contact your church leader and ask for a pastoral visit. It's what they do every day.

4) When the crisis moment has passed, reflect on how you felt and why. If you felt close to snapping even just once, you must get yourself more support. Tell your family that you need some more support to get through this difficult patch. Ask for more frequent visits from your health visitor – it's what they do all the time. Look at what triggered your emotion so that you can recognise times when you may be more vulnerable, and if possible avoid the triggers.

Above all, don't isolate yourself. Ask for some help and company.

Shaking babies
Shaking babies can result in blindness, deafness, brain damage or death.

I can't get the birth out of my head

Whether you had a normal birth or an assisted one, the chances are it was an experience of intense emotion, effort and pain. It is entirely normal to have it churning around your head while you make sense of the huge event that has occurred. However much you prepared for the event, even if you've had a baby before, it's likely that the whole experience was different from what you expected. For some of us, the rawness of the memory softens over time and it settles easily into our memory banks. For others of us, particularly those whose births didn't work out as planned, the memory and accompanying emotions just won't leave us alone.

> *I felt like a CD that had jammed and was playing the same high-pitched squeal of my birth experience, over and over again.*
>
> (Michelle, 24)

I had similar struggles after my first birth, even dissolving into tears at the sound of passing sirens as they reminded me of the emergency rush to get my baby out. I had a chat with my pastor, who prayed with me and also gave me a few techniques to get my Technicolor memories under control.

Keeping your birth memories in check

Tip number 1:

Focus on the birth memory that keeps bothering you, and then, as if you're looking through a camera lens, zoom it in and out, in and out. You're in charge of how fast or slowly you zoom in and out. This technique definitely started to give me a sense of being in charge of my memories.

Tip number 2:

In your imagination, roll the troublesome memory up into a ball and throw it from hand to hand. Then throw it off a hill and watch it bounce away into the distance.

Tip number 3:

Look at your mental picture of your troublesome memory.

Then, in your imagination, dress the people in the scene in fancy dress. Yes, even the obstetricians. Then in your mind's eye add some funky music to the scene.

It's amazing how simply playing around with a memory can take away the power it had over you. It starts to become a memory that doesn't snag you with a cocktail of emotions every time it springs into your head. Sounds crazy, but playing around with the memory helped me regain a sense of perspective. Yes, the birth was traumatic, but it is over now. Finished. A memory just like any other memory. I was free to move on from the experience. Many women find it really helpful to talk through their birth experience with someone who was there. Then any forgotten parts can be filled in, and the general emotion of the experience shared with someone. Debriefing is sometimes a really important part of being able to move on with your life and enjoy your new-found motherhood.

I'm bored!

This one is not difficult to sort out. If it's the monotony of baby care that has bored you, then there's not much I can say. Sometimes things just have to be done, and that's that. In the land of parenthood the reward for all your efforts is not usually seen for years. Even then, there is no guarantee of how much appreciation you'll get. As your baby develops, you will have more interaction, which makes all the difference.

Having a baby is certainly no reason to let your brain vegetate. Take up a new hobby, visit some new places with baby on your back or write a book. Teach yourself Japanese/cordon-bleu cookery or start a home business. Having a baby has been the catalyst for many women to start a whole new career that fits around home life.

Time out with your Father God

Sometimes life just wears us out. We find ourselves slumped on the sofa, tired, drained and empty. This paragraph is for those days, when we've just had enough. The days when we don't feel like talking to anyone, or when we know we've made a mistake, or when we wish life was different. Even talking to God feels like too much hard work.

Well how about... if the hard-work part of talking to God was cancelled, and you didn't even have to come into his presence on your own? How would it be if he wasn't inviting you to glumly discuss your failings, but to come to a party?

> He has taken me to the banquet hall, and his banner over me is love (Song of Songs 2:4).

This is the verse stuck on my fridge for those dull days. Why? Well, "he brought me..." means I don't have to drag myself to God on my own. Like Cinderella going to the ball, Jesus himself clothes me in beauty and dignity and escorts me to the party of his presence.

But what about how I've failed him, not talked to him for ages?

Here's the really special bit... "His banner over me is love". I don't have a banner over me saying "Could do better" or "Made lots of mistakes". The banner over my head isn't even about what I could be in the future. It's the banner God holds over my head right now, just as I am. "Love". Look in a mirror and say to yourself, "I am loved and lovely in the eyes of God". It's true. Copy it out, stick it on the fridge and say it every day, especially on the grey days.

Chapter 12   # Fridge Ministry for New Mums

I've got a fairly large fridge door; it's where I stick the things that matter. You know, like money-off coupons for Häagen-Dazs™ ice cream, the directions to my favourite accessories shop; essential stuff. I also stick on it things that have significance to me, such as scriptures, quotes and wise words I come across. I stick them on my fridge, rather than in my Bible or a pretty notebook, because I want them to have an impact on my everyday life. Not just for "feel-good moments" when I open a frilly notebook. My fridge words of encouragement are for the good days, the hard days and the grey days.

Here's the fun bit... Get scissors and cut out your favourite nuggets of wisdom from the following pages and stick them on your fridge! What's the point of having a moment of encouragement/inspiration/blessing when you read a book, then closing it when you've finished, and carrying on with life where you left off? That's the key to knowing God's touch as you have a baby – the reason for this book. It's about God being with you, affecting your heart, calling your name in your day-to-day life. As you drive to work, pick up the kids' toys, grab some milk from the fridge. Allow the Lord of lords to dine with you; let him in.

I originally thought having a "study guide" for this section. But let's be honest... Who has time to spare for an exhaustive study guide when there's a sale at the baby shop, your friend's hen night and a rerun of *Frasier* all vying for your attention? Instead, I've cobbled together bite-sized chunks of blessing – snippets and hot tips from *Dear Lord, I Feel Like a Whale!* that you can dip into when you please and stick on the fridge. The second section contains amazing true-life stories of women whom I badgered into putting the details down on paper.

Fridge stick-ons are the new black... Get your scissors, and let's do it!

Bite-sized chunks from Chapter 1: "Oops, I Told the Doughnut-seller"

Being pregnant gives you a sense that anything is possible.

Tempting as it was to slob around the house all day swigging neat antacid and reading baby magazines, I decided to spend some time seeking God.

Finding out that you're pregnant brings with it a kind of thrill/ panic combination that reminds me of the exhilarating yet scary rush of childhood adventures.

How does my baby's heart start beating?
How does each cell know what it is to become?
Why is there new life?
Could it be possible that God longs for this baby even more than I do?

Until I did that test I had no clue that there was a whole new life growing inside me. God alone knew his treasured secret.

Armed with such exciting thoughts, it can be tempting to imagine that you will give birth to a serene little article who grows up to love church more than chocolate and wants to be the next Billy Graham or Mother Teresa. Indeed, you may be one of the lucky few. The rest of us find ourselves with a wriggling, sleep-defying individual who grows up wanting to be an astronaut.

No guts, no glory.

It's not too late to be what you could have been.

Eternal life isn't pie in the sky when you die; it's steak on the plate while you wait.

Bite-sized chunks from Chapter 2: Stockpiling Mum-wisdom

She (mother) is their earth... she is their food and their bed and the extra blanket when it grows cold in the night; she is their warmth and their health and their shelter.

You are your baby's universe. It is impossible to grasp your value to him.

It takes courage to be a parent. Trust your instinct, make use of some stockpiled wisdom, and then go for it.

A wise mother is not so much one who can calm a crying baby or toilet-train a toddler, but one who can hold on to peace when there is chaos all around.

If you invest yourself in your family, you are very likely to turn around your family's destiny.

Bite-sized chunks from Chapter 3: Beauty in Pregnancy: Not Mission Impossible

A definite bonus of being pregnant is that you'll have a nice set of boobs for a while.

God calls me beautiful not for what I look like, or even for what I might become. God calls me beautiful because I am his.

You will be a crown of splendour in the LORD's hand... (Isaiah 62:3).

... Mother [is] all-enveloping, protective, nourishing. Mother is food; she is love; she is warmth; she is earth. To be loved by her means to be alive, to be rooted, to be at home.

(Erich Fromm 1900–1980)

Bite-sized chunks from Chapter 4: What If...?

The world shouts at us to get self-esteem by being pleased with who we are. Actually, real self-confidence is being pleased with who God says we are.

The true strength of a woman is in the tenderness of her heart.

Having a baby can be the start of the slippery slope to becoming a nagging wife. Don't let it happen!

My lover spoke and said to me, "Arise, my darling, my beautiful one, and come with me" (Song of Songs 2:10).

The woman in the Song of Songs revelled in the love of her life. Her words show just how we can enjoy the company of Jesus, our "lover".

Trusting in God is not a way of calling down a blanket ban on all unpleasant experiences.

Children are a gift. I cannot control a gift. I cannot dictate when it will arrive or what it will be like. I can only receive it with thanks.

The one who is shaping your little one is the very same one who flung the stars into space, moved mountains and raised the dead.

Come to me, all you who are weary and burdened, and I will give you rest (Matthew 11:28).

Bite-sized chunks from Chapter 5: Maybe It's Time We Got a Scalextric...

Everything, when you're expecting a baby, is seen through pregnancy-tinted glasses.

The classic male approach to pregnancy is:
One of awe (at the sheer size of your breasts)
One of fear (have you SEEN the film *Aliens*?)
One of moderate/extreme concern (for your well-being, not for whether he'll ever have sex again).

Common sentence-starters to avoid when you're talking to your man:

"I know you're not interested, but..."

"I hope you're not going to do that when we've got a baby."

"I'm the one going through this, you know."

"You've got absolutely no idea what I'm going through."

Fatherhood was God's idea. The father of a child is worthy of respect from those around him.

Fatherhood has always represented hope and a future. That is why there are so many meticulous lists of paternity in the Old Testament. "So-and-so-begat-so-and-so..."

His fragile sense of honour in becoming a father could quite easily be smothered by a pregnant wife who demands something akin to subservience to her, the pregnant one.

Daddy-to-be:

He has honour because God has called him to be a father.

He is brave because God will never leave him.

He has vision because God has given him hope.

He can do anything if his wife believes in him.

Wedding Vows

Why wait till your silver anniversary to renew them together?

Bite-sized chunks from Chapter 6: The Joy of Labour

OK, so now I have your attention. Calling a chapter "The Agony of Labour" might not have been quite as enticing. Maybe I should have called it "It's not over till the Fat Lady sings". I don't know about you, but for me the "fat" jokes are wearing a bit thin after nine months of girth.

Anyone found the "off" button yet?

However difficult the delivery, the miracle of birth can never be diluted.

There is pain at times of great passion. God didn't make a race of robots.

I wonder if God shouted in the heavens as he created the world...

In the Old Testament, God's people gave cries of victory and blew on their horns as they advanced into new territory. Embarking on parenthood is entering uncharted territory too. I think labour is a fitting time to cry out to the Lord.

Bite-sized chunks from Chapter 7: How to Have a Delicious, Inspiring Home (God in the House!)

Let's be peace-chasers rather than lifestyle-chasers.

When it snows, she has no fear for her household; for all of them are clothed in scarlet (Proverbs 31:21).

O sweet Jesus, touch our hearts. Let our words be like rivers of honey through our homes. Soften our hearts.

Bite-sized chunks from Chapter 8: Making Good Choices is Easier than You Think

In the sheltered simplicity of the first days after a baby is born, one sees again the magical closed circle, the miraculous sense of two people existing only for each other.

(Anne Morrow Lindbergh, b. 1901)

Does it have God's fingerprints on it?

A time to search and a time to give up, a time to keep and a time to throw away... (Ecclesiastes 3:6).

Let's not be earwigs when it comes to decision-making! Let's not ignore the possible consequences of our choices.

The issue is not so much whether there is an outside job or interest in the schedule, but what's most important in the schedule.

Now is your time to love your husband, your children and your home with every ounce of passion that you have.

If you really have no choice but to work when you have a little one, do it as well as mothering. Not *instead of* mothering. You are a precious resource.

Beauty in nature is closely interwoven with order. I suspect that if we submit ourselves to God's priorities for our life, the beauty only glimpsed in a snowflake or a rainbow will be ours in full measure.

Order, routine and structure are actually liberating. They give shape and structure to the rich pattern of life. Order and creativity go hand in hand.

Bite-sized chunks from Chapter 9: Life with a New Baby (The Real Story!)

Tender, raw, intimate, overwhelming weeks. Precious days. Never let the blunt edge of tiredness distract you from the miracle in your arms.

Should you be daft enough to look in the mirror, you may notice that the gravity fairy has paid you a surprise visit.

I know for certain that a sense of ease rather than unease is actually in the new-mum blessing pack, should you choose to share the weight of early baby weeks with your Father God.

Part of the knack of successfully negotiating the first six weeks with a baby is not to have unrealistically high expectations of things. Then, if you find yourself with the blues/after-pains/rocket-boobs combination in your lap, it's still a pain but it doesn't get quite the same grip on your psyche as if you had thought life would be normal once the baby was born.

"Let go and let God." OK, it certainly is a corny bumper sticker. Not a bad idea, though.

I had half a dozen baby books informing me how to whip up a mean pecan and lime purée, or how to do origami with a piece of terry-towelling. I even had a book explaining how you could use sign language to communicate with babies. (I got quite into this one until the Greek lady across the road thought I was making obscene gestures.) I've since learned that it doesn't really matter whether I can do any of these things. What babies and children need as much as love is to be accepted by their parents. Accepted just as they are.

I will take refuge in the shadow of your wings (Psalm 57:1).

Sometimes the demands and strains of the early weeks can feel like toiling in a desert under constant blazing heat. The early weeks are intense; each moment is new and exhilaration often walks hand in hand with despair. Psalm 57:1 was my answer to the incessant effort of the early weeks with a baby. Someone to bring a cool breeze to the hot, weary nights. As I nestled, cuddled and protected my little one, so I came to Father God and nestled myself in him.

Bite-sized chunks from Chapter 10: Feeding Babies (What the Leaflets Don't Tell You)

The top ten reasons to breastfeed

1. Breast milk contains all the nutrients and water your baby needs.
2. It reduces the risk of infections and allergies during childhood.
3. It reduces the cancer risk for mum.
4. It's a unique bonding experience.
5. It's free.
6. It burns up mum's spare calories, which means you lose that "baby belly" more quickly.
7. You don't have the hassle of buying/preparing formula and sterilising bottles.
8. Once you get used to it, you can feed anywhere. Your life does not revolve around "feed times".
9. The milk adapts to the baby's needs as she grows.
10. It's a brilliant, quick comforter for an unsettled baby – night or day.

What if the "WHAT IF" worries didn't call the shots any more?

The silver spoons of breastfeeding

1) Good position – baby facing you, with both of you comfortable. Have one hand supporting baby's head and the
   other holding the breast.
2) Latching on – wait for that brief moment when the baby's
   mouth is open wide then swiftly move baby's mouth to
   the nipple; if she doesn't get a real mouthful, ease her off
   and try again.
3) Feed often – this is such hard work at first but it is the
   only way to build up your milk supply; she will settle into
   a pattern when she is ready.

Pause, focus, cherish, feed.
Cherishing comes from the heart, not a breast or a bottle.

"Enclave" – make feeding time a special cherishing time for
the two of you. Whether breastfeeding or bottle-feeding, this
is intimate time. She delights in her mummy and her
mummy delights in her. The King of kings delights in you
both and adorns you with flowers of his blessing.

You have a unique role in your child's life. You are mummy.

Bite-sized chunks from Chapter 11: "It's Not Supposed to Be Like This!"

Five days after a C-section I congratulated myself on how well
I was doing as I humped the turbo-smacking vacuum up the
stairs. Three days later I was whizzing round to my friends'
houses, baby and toddler in tow, showing off my baby. In the
evenings I stayed up as late as the rest of the adult world as I
didn't want to "miss out" (on what I'm still not sure)... Stop
the supermum train! I want to get off!

Going for a run is supposed to be one of the best ways of relieving stress. If someone can prise me away from the fridge, I might give it a try one day!

Ten ways to soothe a crying baby
1) Feed her (even if you've only just finished feeding her).
2) Carry her around with you in a baby sling.
3) Be on the move.
4) Go for a wander around the garden.
5) Music. A familiar song is especially good for settling the babies who are overtired.
6) Scripture. Speaking words from the Bible over your baby is one of the best things you can ever do.
7) Comforter. Little ones have special bonds with their favourite toy or blanket.
8) Triple shimmy with a twist. It's a mystery, but daddies hold the monopoly on the art of baby-rocking. Whether daddy wants to do his rocking bit at 3am is another matter.
9) Pacifier/dummy/soother. This one's down to personal choice, like many things on the jungle track of parenthood.
10) Feed her again.

Chapter 13   True Stories from Fellow Mums

Imagine that a delivery boy were to knock on your door with two huge parcels for you. The first parcel, tied with shiny pink ribbon, contains all the neatly sanitised advice anyone could possibly need for having a baby and starting a family. The second parcel, tied with rainbow ribbon, is a bit battered and worn around the edges, but contains real advice and stories written by new mums and older mums. Pitfalls to avoid, sanity-saving tips, that sort of thing. Which box do you rip open first?

I know my choice, hands down. So here it is – real stories and tips from mums: unwrapped!

*   *   *

"Having my girls has taken me to highs I've never previously experienced. Looking at other people's children is wonderful but it doesn't touch this. To watch my own children become, from the tiniest spark of life in my womb, is unfathomable. Here we are with two beautiful, captivating children with bag loads of personality, humour, the desire to love others and the capacity for so much learning and exploration. And all this from us! No, not all this from us. This has to be God. When he touched my life in this way I was changed forever and will always be rich."

(Helen, 31, mum to Megan and Dawn)

"Five years ago, when I was exactly 25 weeks pregnant, I went into premature labour for no apparent reason. My husband took me to the hospital after I had had stomach pains for three hours. After an examination I was told that I was 4cm dilated and it was too late to stop the labour. I had a placental abruption. Joseph was born by emergency Caesarean section and rushed to the neonatal unit immediately; he had a 40% chance of survival because he survived the labour. I recall wiping my husband's tears away and saying, 'Don't worry, the Lord knows. It will be alright.'

The neonatal doctors nearly lost Joe several times, and we spent $4^{1}/_{2}$ months in hospital. Many people around the world were praying for my son. On one occasion there was a real problem, as very little oxygen was getting to his brain. I ran to phone my husband, who was at church. He told the pastor, who called everyone back into the church to pray.

I went into the neonatal unit bathroom and got down on my knees. As I sobbed I begged Jesus for my son's life – if it was his will. I went back to the neonatal ward and was told that all was well now. I told the consultant that this was because my church had prayed for Joseph. These sort of scenarios happened many times.

One Friday I was shown an X-ray of Joe's collapsed lung. Again the church prayed. On Monday they took another X-ray, and the lung was normal. I saw it with my own eyes. My Jesus had touched him again.

God used me while I was there to minister to several mums, and encourage them. I prayed for their babies. 'How can you be so nice,' I was asked, 'when your baby is one of the sickest in the unit?' 'I have Jesus,' I told the new mum.

After 16 weeks of expressing my milk and feeding by tube, I could at last breastfeed him, and Joe and I went home. He was not on oxygen, as we had been warned the week before. Again Jesus undertook for Joe's needs. Joe is now a healthy five-year-old with no problems. I remember when I was all alone at night with Joe, all visitors gone – my Jesus was still there. I can never forget him, the one who held my hand through it all."

(Angela, mum to Joe, 5)

"God has shown me that my four children are only on loan to us and that he has only entrusted them to our care for a short while. I take great comfort from this, as it helps me to know that I am doing this 'job' for him and therefore need to give my best."

(Danielle Vaughan, mum to Farley, Liberty, Jemima and Reuben)

"Soothing crying babies – with both of mine, if I gently patted their bottoms (obviously with nappy on!) when they were crying this seemed to soothe them.

Has being a mum been different from what I thought it would be? Yes, definitely! I don't think I ever really realised what a sacrifice becoming a mum would mean for my life, my dreams, etc. To a degree, I think all mums naïvely think that their children will fit around them, and be these perfect little people, whereas in reality everything goes out the window, I never dreamt that I'd be spending almost five years in crèche nearly every Sunday! My time has virtually disappeared, and time for my husband (a church pastor) is often short and sparse. About a year ago I was really struggling with this, as I felt like 'me' as a person had disappeared; I was Mummy, I was a wife, I was a pastor's wife, I was cleaner, chef, counsellor, etc, but where had the real 'me' gone? Then I felt like God reminded me that this was for a season of my life, like we go through 'spiritual seasons'. Inside I felt like it was winter, but

I think God was showing me that it was spring. Before I know it these little blossoms of mine are going to flower into the people they are going to be, and then part of me will yearn for them to be little buds again, because when they get to 11–12 years old, Mum and Dad will not be the 'coolest' people for them to hang out with! They are such a precious gift, and I wouldn't want to be without them."

(Lyn Hallewell, mum to Ben and Grace)

"Although my pregnancy was unexpected, I was pleased about it. Overnight, though, when I was eight weeks pregnant, I became very low indeed, although at the time I thought I was quite sane, and everyone else had the problem! I couldn't stand to be in the same room as my husband; I didn't want to look at him, hear him, or have him touch me, and I didn't want his baby. My moods were very up and down, and I was very irrational. Within a week I'd told my husband he'd have to move out, and that I wanted a divorce. Reluctantly, he moved out, thinking that some space would help things to settle. It didn't. Nothing changed with me; I wanted him out of my life. My husband is a church pastor, and the church gave him paid leave so that he could go and stay with some friends in Winnipeg, Canada. His whole world had just fallen apart. Inside me there was a real wrestle going on; spiritually, I think there was a battle going on over me. My friends stood by me, and never said that they agreed with what was going on, but never said that they disapproved either – that was important: they were there to listen to me, and to pray with me, but never to judge. I was utterly convinced that I was fine; I continued to go to church as normal and my faith in God never altered.

The day my husband flew to Canada things started to change, and I think God really started to break through. I can't remember exactly what I was doing at the time, but I realised how awful I'd been to my husband, and cried and cried, thinking that I had lost him. I remembered a verse that someone had given us on our wedding day (Jeremiah 29:11–14a), and realised that I had to go out to Canada to save our marriage. A dear friend paid for my flight. I returned home when I was 14 weeks pregnant, my husband a week later. The day he returned I had my first ultrasound scan – that was a very emotional and precious moment. I am so thankful to God. When I was 20 weeks pregnant I was reading an article in a mother-and-baby magazine about the 'new taboo', antenatal depression, and as I read I felt as if someone was writing about me – the symptoms exactly matched what I had experienced in early pregnancy. It took a while for the wounds to heal, but five years later we're very happily married, with two children, and we recently renewed our wedding vows."

(Lyn)

"The second time God met me during my pregnancy was in my third trimester. Before I became pregnant I had gone through a period when I was fearful of death, something which I thought I had sorted out, but as I came near to my due date, these fears rose again. One day I came across the Holman Hunt picture *The Light of the World*. I was captivated by the picture and put it up at home. I'd often just look at the picture, which is of Jesus standing holding a lamp, knocking at a door covered in thorns and weeds, surrounded by dark woodland (the idea being that Jesus knocks on our hearts, and if we let him in he lights up our life). Through looking at the picture and meditating, I realised that Jesus lives in me, and I am always going to be with him, and he is always going to be with me; I'm not going to be left out in the woods somewhere.

When I went into labour I visualised this picture with every contraction, and just called out to God and tried to meditate. I really felt God's peace with me. I went on to have a seven-and-a-half hour labour, which is quite short for a first-time mum, and only used gas and air, no forceps, stitches, etc. I really felt that God was with me."

(Lyn)

"During my second pregnancy we were told, following our first scan, that they were unable to locate a stomach in the baby; we went for a more detailed scan at around 23 weeks, and again they confirmed that they could not locate a stomach. My midwife arranged for me to go to hospital and see a specialist, but told us that we'd have to prepare ourselves, as it looked like the baby would need major surgery within hours of being born, as it seemed that the oesophagus and stomach were not joined together – hence why they couldn't find a stomach on the ultrasound. Our appointment came through and I was to have the scan at 27 weeks' gestation. My husband and I worked for a Vineyard church in Vancouver, Canada at the time, as assistant pastors. Two days before the scan, during a church service, the senior pastor's wife, turned round and put her hands on my stomach. 'God has just told me that he has healed your baby, and that he wants me to pray for it,' she said to me. I was shocked, but part of me also thought, 'Right, we'll see!' Tuesday morning I went for my scan with my husband. It was tense, waiting to be seen. They got me to lie on a couch by an ultrasound monitor, and had a look at the baby. As soon as they put the ultrasound on my stomach, they said, 'Oh, there's a stomach there, alright.'

My husband and I cried. We are so sure that our little girl was healed in the womb by God. Praise the Lord."

(Lyn)

"The best bits about being a mum are the little things: holding hands as we go for a walk, the smile and hug I get first thing in the morning. I love to see the expressions of joy and wonder that cross his face when he first sees something new, something to which my senses are often dulled by the familiarity of it all – until I see it afresh through the eyes of this child. I love the way he sees the details in the scene and shows me the little gems that my eye must have seen but my brain did not notice in the overall picture. There is such an amazing sense of privilege at watching as he grows up, learning new things, developing in so many ways and enjoying the adventure along the way.

Then, at the end of the day, there is that extra-special part of being a mum which is watching him sleeping and feeling overwhelmed by the love I feel for this little, amazing person – my son!"

(Shelma Vaughan)

"I could write hundreds of pages on where I went wrong and just a few on maybe where I went right when bringing up the children. But, sifting through the caverns of my mind, one thing always, always, always looms large, and that is TO SPEND AS MUCH TIME WITH YOUR CHILD OR CHILDREN AS POSSIBLE, NOT JUST AT BEDTIME, BUT GOOD-QUALITY, INVESTED TIME. IT WILL PAY DIVIDENDS. SORRY ABOUT THE CAPITALS, BUT I HAVE LEARNED THAT YOU ONLY REALISE WHEN THEY HAVE GOT UP AND FLOWN THE NEST WHAT A SHORT TIME YOU REALLY HAD WITH THEM – YOU CAN'T CLAIM IT BACK."

(Pauline White, children now aged 27 and 31 years)

"I remember promising in church 'for better or for worse', but I had no idea that when I became a mother the 'better' would hit such high notes and the 'worse' could look so black.

When I became pregnant with my second child I had no idea what lay before me. I suffered from SPD (where the pelvis separates) and was in pain from six weeks pregnant! By 20 weeks I could no longer walk without crutches and at 28 weeks I was in a wheelchair. My husband cared for me and for our daughter, Emily, whom I could no longer look after alone.

Joseph, being expected to be a big baby, was induced at 37 weeks; 9lb 9oz he weighed in at, so it seemed like a good decision to assist his arrival! Everything seemed perfect: Emily adored her new brother; David and I were enjoying our expanded family; the midwife came for the seven-day check and our little boy was doing wonderfully.

Day eight dawned and seemed like any other. Joseph slept peacefully all morning; he wasn't terribly interested in lunch, and as the afternoon wore on we began to be concerned. By tea time we still couldn't keep him awake; he ate nothing, and we were worried.

Our doctor was clearly worried about Joseph, because he went pale and floppy, was unresponsive and began to make a very high-pitched moan. Every fibre of my body hurt as I wheeled myself around (still unable to walk from the SPD). Joseph was X-rayed; the doctors performed a lumbar puncture, where they take fluid from the spine, to check that he didn't have bacterial meningitis.

Joseph was admitted, monitored, fed through a nose tube and that night was the longest of our lives. I can remember sitting watching my tiny baby sleep and praying, 'O God please don't take him; eight days is not enough'.

I couldn't manage any more words than that; I'm sure the medical staff thought I was a little strange as I sang hymns to this tiny baby, but I had to do something. I felt so helpless, so powerless, and so small. This tiny baby depended on me for everything and suddenly there was nothing I could do.

Our stay in hospital lasted five days, Joseph had viral meningitis but he pulled through; after that first 24 hours we began to see very tiny improvements and by the third day I began to believe it might actually be alright.

I learned a lot about God's love for me and my children that night. I felt God's assurance in a way I cannot explain. I knew what it meant in the Bible when it says the Spirit 'groans' for us when we have no words to pray.

I grasped a sense of God's vastness and my own helplessness, as I sat beside the hospital bed; on the back of a soup packet I wrote these words that seemed to express what it means to me to be a Christian mum:

Ours for a while

I gaze down at this tiny bundle
Nestled in my arms right now
I cannot help but wipe my eyes
And wonder Why? and How?

How could something so perfect
Be trusted to our care
Beautifully, wonderfully formed and made
Each nail, each breath, each hair

Then there came the answer
I've entrusted him to both of you
You hold him for a little while
Mummy and Daddy too

But ultimately, he is mine
For I moulded him, formed his fingers and toes
I placed the sparkle in his eyes
And shaped his tiny nose

My hand will be on him
For all his days on earth
I will stay and walk with him
As I promised before his birth."

(Alison Booker)

"It must be wonderful for a woman, whilst she is pregnant, to realise that the child she is carrying is a gift from God. To be able to read Psalm 139 and realise that the Lord has every moment of her child's life planned and that she can trust him in every aspect of her pregnancy. I, unfortunately, did not have this privilege when I had my sons, as I didn't become a Christian until they were six and eight, but God's timing is perfect, and as they have grown up (being 16 and 18 now) we have seen the hand of the Lord in every part of our lives. What I would like to share, as a mother, are a couple of incidents in the life of my eldest son (who committed his life to the Lord when he was ten) that illustrate the gracious way our Lord answers prayers and gives evidences to children of his mighty power.

When our son was ten, he started senior school, and part of his school equipment was a fountain pen, something that he had not had to use in junior school. The ink cartridge was quite novel to him, and one day, after filling his pen, he decided to spin around the room, holding his pen aloft – without the lid on! You can guess what happened next! Ink spattered all over the wallpaper in the living room, or at least a large section by the hearth. He and I were horrified; what would his dad say? We sat down together on the floor and decided to ask the Lord about what to do. After a couple of minutes I was able to say to him that God had given me the answer – to dab a weak solution of bleach on the offending patches with a piece of cotton wool, and it worked. As soon as I had managed to remove all of the ink, we again sat down together and thanked the Lord for his goodness.

A year or so later, his hamster, Sherwood, went missing and he was very anxious about it. We hunted high and low for Sherwood, but to no avail, and my son went to sleep very dejected. Before he settled down for the night we prayed together and asked God to look after Sherwood and help us to find him. Early the next morning I went into my son's room and sat down by his wardrobe and prayed. Whilst I was praying I heard a scratching noise by his window and went over to investigate. He had a couple of loose floorboards in that part of his room and I lifted one to discover dear little Sherwood underneath. I woke my son up and gently we lifted Sherwood out of the hole and put him back into his cage, but not before we had discovered that Sherwood's cheeks were bulging; he turned out to have a Subbuteo ball in one cheek and a marble in the other! Again, we thanked God for the answer to our prayers.

To me, this was a clear demonstration to my young son that God does answer prayer. Our son is now 18, at university, and still trusting in the Lord and seeing him answering prayer in his life and in the lives of others. What a wonderful God we serve."

(Bernadette Mason)

"Nathaniel's birth story:

We planned a hospital birth, and we prayed asking Father God to give us the right midwives. We were allocated a team with the theory that we would then get a familiar midwife during labour. This was not to be. Labour began at two in the morning but we managed until seven o'clock before calling the number we had, which turned out to be someone's home number. She was cross. We tried another number but repeatedly got answerphones. Eventually, at ten o'clock a midwife phoned and said she was horrified to think that no one had contacted me yet and apologised that she was not from my team, but could she help? Without warning, she turned up on the doorstep fifteen minutes later. Because she was an unexpected and an unfamiliar face, my contractions, which had been coming every five minutes for hours, came to a complete halt. Thankfully they resumed after about half an hour.

It turned out that she was a godsend and exactly the lady we had prayed for – she was a Christian, and had been a missionary in Asia close to where my husband and I had been brought up. So we 'clicked' and she prayed over us during labour, and of course we felt free to pray out loud too. She was extremely professional and respected our every wish on the birth plan. What a wonderful facilitation of the most profound and exhilarating experience of birth for the three of us.

The next day in the hospital, another divine arrangement came to pass – a midwife who had also been a missionary and had worked in the Indian hospital where my darling husband was born, came to see us on her rounds! We were bowled over by God's goodness to us in setting up these two dear instrumental ladies for us. His faithfulness endures forever. We were so grateful for his favour. Our baby was born with Cystic Fibrosis, so before feeling called to become a mother of two instead of one, I asked the Father for a girl without CF..."

(Annie, mum to Nathaniel, Corrie and Gracie)

"Corrie's birth story:

Part of my nesting instinct meant that I had to feel ready for labour, so as well as asking midwives all my questions and making last-minute curtains, I wrote out scripture verses to carry us through the birth process. I made a large poster, which I put on the wall in my birthing room (our lounge at home). It had a variety of expressions – life-giving, anxiety-reducing, trust and confidence in the Lord. My dear husband could declare these truths over us during labour. I also had a piece of card with Bible verses on, for me to hold onto at times of need.

I was thirteen days overdue; the next day was the deadline for induction discussions and possibly 'goodbye home birth'. Father God knew that the home birth was important to me, and I knew that he knew. It was Sunday evening. I waddled down to the front row at church to make sure I could bask in God's presence and connect with him at this spiritually significant time. We sang a worship song; 'His banner over me is love', and I sensed that this was the tool the Father was giving me to take with me into labour.

I said to him, 'Father, it would be so good if I could have a good night's sleep and labour could begin in the morning', and that is exactly what he gifted me with. At 7am I got out of bed with contractions too uncomfortable to remain lying down.

I repeated the scripture over and over: 'His banner over me is love'. My darling husband questioned 'spanner?, you want a spanner?' I guess he was prepared for his wife saying strange things during labour! Corrie was born in the water, a whopping 9lb 7oz. We enjoyed breastfeeding together on the sofa as we recovered from the birth. What a special way to rejoin after the umbilical cord has so recently been severed."

(Annie, mum to Nathaniel, Corrie and Gracie)

"Gracie's birth story:

I was so deeply ministered to by my midwife's listening skills – way above my need for her to be medically informed was my need to be heard – she listened to all my worries and they seemed to evaporate as soon as I felt heard. She had a deep respect for the natural course of labour and birth and seemed magically to put me at ease. Her reassuring presence enabled me to enter into a new depth of relaxation. I surrendered to the powerful process of labour, safe in the hands of God's love – the creator, the great midwife, author of life. My sister-in-law, Rosie, was also supporting me through that long night, and her listening and attentive presence was an enormous help to me. Oh, to celebrate the gathering around of women supporting women in their deep experience of bringing forth new life! The lights were dim, candles flickered peacefully, the water was reflecting and the lush plants nearby set the scene for tranquillity.

The contractions intensified and I began pacing back and forth until I finally entered the pool; a huge relief swept over me as the warm water lapped around me and my precious load. My darling husband Simon had just stepped out of the room to go and change into his shorts to get into the pool with me when all of a sudden the urge to push overwhelmed me and I cried out, 'I need to push!' He was called back – there was no time to change so he just threw off his shirt and climbed in behind me. The midwives did not even put their hands into the water, allowing nature to take its course. It was important to me to 'breathe the baby out' this time, so after the 'head' was half out and I had felt it, I was surprised when one midwife said, 'Just a little push' – and lo and behold, she slithered slowly out, Simon passed her to me and I heard the midwife say 'It was breech.' I exclaimed, 'What?' She was a surprise breech – thanks be to God, who kept that secret even from an experienced midwife, for, had they known, I would have had to go into hospital and would have lost my dream home-water birth. Apparently, when the bottom (which I had felt but thought was the head) was part-way out, one midwife had thought 'That's a very bald head' before realising that it was not a head at all, but a bottom!

I was absolutely thrilled – what favour he had given me, not only in keeping that surprise but also in giving me an unusual birth. The labour had been long but I had done it without any pain relief apart from TENS™ and the water. I couldn't have asked for more supportive birth attendants. It was an exhilarating experience which I will treasure forever. May God be honoured and glorified through all our lives. Thanks are forever due to his name."

(Annie, mum to Nathaniel, Corrie and Gracie)